The Anti-Great Reset

Building a Better World for All

1

Written by:
Alan E Shields

Copyright © 2023 Alan E Shields

Table of Contents

Introduction:

Unveiling the Shadowy Agenda of "The Great Reset"

In the dimly lit corridors of global power, a sinister plan has emerged, one that threatens the very fabric of society and the global economy. Klaus Schwab, the enigmatic founder of the World Economic Forum (WEF), has unveiled "The Great Reset" with grandiose promises of a transformed world. But beneath the lofty rhetoric lies a web of conspiratorial intentions and a vision that would have dire consequences for us all.

The Great Reset Unmasked

Within the pages of his book and in the secret conclaves of influential elites, Klaus Schwab has outlined a vision for humanity that reeks of control, manipulation, and World domination. "The Great Reset" proposes an audacious overhaul, a cunning scheme to rebuild our societies and economies in the wake of crises. But the devil is in the details, and these details are alarming.

Acknowledging the Hidden Agendas

As the whispers of "The Great Reset" grow louder, so too do the rumblings of discontent and suspicion. Widespread concerns have emerged, shrouded in whispers of hidden agendas. This vision is a guise for centralized control, an insidious plot to strip individuals of their freedoms and autonomy. Property rights, personal liberties, and economic stability are mere collateral damage in this grand conspiracy.

The Purpose of Our Inquiry

This book serves as a beacon in these murky waters, shedding light on the darkest corners of "The Great Reset." It peels back the layers of this covert plan, exposing its sinister components and scrutinizing its malevolent principles. Our journey is not one of passivity but of vigilance, not of acceptance but of defiance.

A Dystopian Vision of Subjugation

Throughout our journey, we emphasize the ominous implications of this agenda. We reveal a vision that threatens individual empowerment, undermines cooperative efforts, and keeps knowledge under lock and key. This is not a world of shared prosperity, but a dystopian realm where opportunity is reserved for the chosen few, and hope is extinguished in the hearts of the masses.

As we shine a light into the darkest recesses of "The Great Reset," let us remember that our collective efforts hold the power to thwart the shadowy designs. Our shared commitment to safeguarding individual freedoms, resisting centralized control, and preserving autonomy is the shield that protects us on this treacherous path. Together, we embark on a journey where we challenge the prevailing agenda, explore alternatives, and, in doing so, erect a bulwark against a world marred by conspiracy— for everyone.

Part I: Debunking the "Great Reset" Narrative

Unraveling the Fear Factor

In the shadows of the world's ever-evolving socio-economic landscape, Klaus Schwab's "The Great Reset" emerges as a beacon for a very few, but for most others, it's a glaring red warning light. The book, which the elites hail as a visionary guide to the future, is seen by 99% of the critical thinkers as a masterclass in the art of fear manipulation.

Schwab's narrative is drenched in a sense of impending doom, urging the world to embrace a new order or face catastrophic consequences. But is this urgency genuine, or is it a calculated move to push a particular agenda? History is replete with examples of leaders and influencers using fear as a tool to control the masses. From the witch hunts of the medieval era to the Red Scare of the 20th century, fear has been a potent weapon in the arsenal of those seeking power.

The "Great Reset" seems to tap into this age-old tactic, painting a picture of a world on the brink, where only a complete overhaul of the system can save us. But at what cost? The narrative subtly hints at the need to sacrifice individual freedoms and autonomy for the 'greater good'. But who defines this 'greater good'? And why should the public, once again, be the ones to pay the price?

The Realities of Stakeholder Capitalism

Schwab's vision of stakeholder capitalism is presented as the antidote to the perceived ills of shareholder capitalism. But is it really the panacea it's made out to be, or just another buzzword-laden concept designed to appease the masses while consolidating power in the hands of a few?

Traditional shareholder capitalism, for all its flaws, has a clear and transparent goal: maximize profits for shareholders. Stakeholder capitalism, on the other hand, purports to consider the interests of all stakeholders, from employees, customers to society at large, and the environment. But herein lies the problem: with so many stakeholders, who gets to decide which interests are prioritized? And more importantly, who holds these decision-makers accountable? This is how they are pushing their ignorant EGS initiative.

While the idea of businesses considering the broader impact of their actions is commendable, the practicality of implementing stakeholder capitalism on a global scale is questionable at best. The potential benefits, such as more equitable wealth distribution and sustainable business practices, are undeniable. However, the drawbacks are equally significant. The ambiguity surrounding the definition of 'stakeholder interests' would lead to decision paralysis, with businesses caught in a never-ending loop of trying to please everyone. Moreover, the shift from a profit-centric model would stifle innovation and economic growth, as businesses become more risk-averse in their quest to appease every stakeholder.

In essence, while stakeholder capitalism sounds like a noble endeavor, its implementation is fraught with challenges. It's essential to critically assess its implications and ensure that it doesn't become just another tool in the hands of global elites to further their interests under the guise of societal betterment.

A Balanced Approach to Sustainable Development

In the labyrinth of global agendas and power plays, Klaus Schwab's "The Great Reset" stands out as a monolithic testament to a vision that, on the surface, seems to champion the cause of sustainable development. But as with many grand visions, the devil is in the details—or perhaps, in what's left unsaid.

Schwab's narrative, while extolling the virtues of environmental protection, often seems to sideline the equally crucial aspect of socio-economic progress. It's as if the world is being asked to choose between the planet and its people. But why can't we have both? Why can't there be a balanced approach that ensures both environmental rejuvenation and socio-economic prosperity?

Intelligent people will argue that the "Great Reset" is less about genuine sustainable development and more about control. By pushing extreme solutions under the banner of environmental protection, we are inadvertently setting ourselves up for a future where the masses are controlled by resource scarcity, while a select few continue to enjoy unchecked power and privilege.

The Role of Democracy

Democracy, the bedrock of modern civilization, finds itself under an insidious threat in Schwab's "Great Reset." While the book doesn't overtly advocate for the dismantling of democratic institutions, the underlying implications are hard to ignore. As of late, the WEF has been pushing to eliminate voting in all countries.

The "Great Reset" envisions a world where decisions are made by a consortium of global entities, corporations, and select, un-elected, individuals. But where does that leave the common man? Where is the representation for the billions who will be most affected by these decisions? The very essence of democracy—of the people, by the people, for the people—seems to be at risk.

It's not hard to imagine a world where, under the guise of global cooperation and sustainable development, power is concentrated in the hands of a few global elites. These elites, operating from their ivory towers, would dictate terms to the rest of the world, eroding the democratic accountability that we hold dear.

The "Great Reset" is trying to be packaged as a vision for a better future, but one must ask: better for whom? As we tread this path, it's crucial to remember that any future devoid of true democratic principles is a future where freedom, choice, and individual rights hang in the balance.

Economic Realities

In the grand tapestry of global economic theories, Klaus Schwab's "The Great Reset" emerges as a perplexing anomaly. While it promises a utopian future of economic stability and shared prosperity, the underlying mechanisms and strategies proposed raise more questions than answers.

At the heart of the "Great Reset" is a radical reshaping of the global economic landscape. But what happens to the job markets when such drastic changes are implemented? Intelligent people would argue that the agenda is a veiled attempt to create a world where automation and AI dominate, pushing millions out of jobs and leading to unprecedented levels of unemployment.

Small businesses, often hailed as the backbone of economies, find no significant mention in Schwab's vision. The "Great Reset" is an orchestrated move to empower multinational corporations while sidelining small enterprises. The potential for increased economic inequality is glaringly evident.

Furthermore, the WEF are paving the way for a new financial system, one that's centralized and devoid of traditional banking mechanisms with their CBDC (Central Bank Digital Currency). Such a shift would have catastrophic implications, leading to a loss of financial autonomy for individuals.

The idea of resource redistribution, while noble on the surface, raises concerns about the actual execution. Will wealth be forcibly taken from some to be given to others? And who decides the deserving recipients? The potential for social unrest and economic upheaval is palpable.

The Hidden Dangers Behind the Digital Currency Push by the WEF

- **Loss of Financial Freedom:**

The allure of Central Bank Digital Currencies (CBDCs) is undeniable. They promise efficiency, transparency, and a modern approach to monetary transactions. But beware, beneath the surface, there lies a potential threat to one of our most cherished freedoms: financial autonomy. The introduction of CBDCs would grant governments, central banks, and some non-elected officials unprecedented access to individual financial activities. While this is touted as a measure for greater security or transparency, it also paves the way for overreach. The very essence of financial freedom is the ability to make choices without undue interference or surveillance. With CBDCs, every transaction, no matter how trivial, would be under the watchful eye of the state, leading many to question: At what cost does this digital evolution come?

- **Selective Payments and Restrictions:**

The very centralized nature of CBDCs would empower authorities to dictate the terms of transactions. Imagine a world where your digital wallet restricts you from buying a book, attending an event, or even donating to a cause. While some might argue that such measures could prevent illegal activities, the broader implications are extremely concerning. The power to enforce economic policies through selective payment restrictions would be a tool for government overreach, definitely stifling freedom of choice and expression. Just image where the system decides that you have bought enough beer for the month and you can no longer buy beer this month. Where would it end?

- **Vulnerability to Political Changes:**

Financial stability often relies on predictability. However, with CBDCs, the rules of the game would change with every shift in political winds. Today's permissible financial behavior might be tomorrow's taboo, depending on the whims of those in power. This vulnerability would lead to an unstable economic environment, where individuals and businesses constantly have to adapt to ever-changing financial regulations and restrictions.

- **Privacy Erosion:**

In a world where data is the new gold, financial privacy becomes even more paramount. CBDCs, unless meticulously designed with stringent privacy measures, would strip away the cloak of anonymity that traditional cash transactions provide. Every purchase, every donation, every financial move would be tracked, logged, and analyzed. This not only raises concerns about personal privacy but also about the potential misuse of such vast amounts of data.

- **Need for Safeguards:**

The challenges posed by CBDCs underscore the urgent need for robust safeguards. While the digital evolution of currency is inevitable, it should not come at the expense of individual freedoms or privacy rights. Crafting a framework that strikes a balance between security, efficiency, and personal liberties will be paramount. As the World Economic Forum and other entities push for the adoption of CBDCs, it's crucial to remember that progress should always be in service of humanity, not at its expense. But we all know that even if there are laws to protect us, nothing can stop them from breaking the laws or changing them at will. That is why using the GlobeTrotter Ecosystem would be the optimal choice.

Cultural and Social Impacts

Culture, an intricate web of shared beliefs, practices, and values, finds itself at a crossroads in the "Great Reset." Schwab's vision, while advocating for global cooperation, seems to inadvertently push for a homogenized global culture.

The potential social impacts of the "Great Reset" are vast and varied. Changes in social norms, driven by a top-down approach, would lead to a world where individuality is suppressed, and conformity is rewarded. Family structures, the bedrock of societies for millennia, would be redefined to fit the new world order. Communities, instead of being organic entities, would become orchestrated setups, devoid of genuine human connections.

One of the most significant concerns is the potential erasure of diverse cultural identities. In a world driven by the "Great Reset," is there room for the rich tapestry of cultures, languages, and traditions that have evolved over centuries? People should argue that the agenda is a covert attempt to create a monolithic global culture, where dissenting voices are silenced, and individual identities are submerged in a sea of enforced uniformity.

Technological Challenges

In the digital age, technology stands as both our greatest ally and potential adversary. Klaus Schwab's "The Great Reset" paints a picture of a world seamlessly integrated through cutting-edge technology. But as we delve deeper into this vision, unsettling questions arise.

Emerging technologies, from AI to blockchain, are central to the "Great Reset" agenda. But who controls these technologies? Intelligent people would argue that beneath the veneer of progress lies a sinister plot to harness these tools for surveillance and control. The promise of a connected world suddenly feels like a dystopian nightmare where every move is watched, every dissent noted. Picture The Hunger Games and that will give you a good idea of their vision.

Data privacy, a fundamental right in many democracies, seems to be on the chopping block. The "Great Reset" hints at a world where personal data is freely traded among corporations and governments, turning individuals into mere data points. The idea of a digital ID, while convenient, raises alarms about the potential for misuse. This would be a covert method to track and control global populations.

The narrative champions technology as a tool for empowerment, but the underlying tone suggests otherwise. Instead of being tools to enhance human potential, there's a looming threat that these technologies will be wielded to suppress and dominate.

Globalization and National Sovereignty

The age-old debate between globalization and national sovereignty finds itself at the epicenter of the "Great Reset." Schwab's vision of a globally integrated world seems to come at the cost of individual national identities and autonomy.

While global cooperation is undeniably essential in addressing challenges, does it warrant the dissolution of national borders? Intelligent people should see this as a ploy to establish a one-world government, where power is concentrated in the hands of a few, and the unique identities of nations are erased.

The erosion of national borders, as proposed in the "Great Reset," would lead to a loss of sovereignty. Nations, instead of being independent entities with their own cultures, laws, and governance, would most likely become mere provinces in a global empire. The potential for cultural erasure, loss of democratic rights, and the imposition of a singular global agenda is palpable.

In the tug-of-war between globalization and national sovereignty, the "Great Reset" seems to be pulling hard in one direction. But at what cost? The vision of a united world is undoubtedly appealing, but not if it means the loss of the rich diversity, traditions, and freedoms that nations hold dear.

"You Will Own Nothing"

One of the most provocative statements associated with the World Economic Forum's vision for 2030 is the idea that "You will own nothing, and you'll be happy." But what does this truly mean for the individual and society at large?

The concept of ownership is deeply ingrained in human psyche and societal structures. It's a symbol of success, security, and autonomy. To suddenly propose a world where personal ownership is a thing of the past raises eyebrows and fuels conspiracy theories. This is a covert attempt to strip individuals of their rights and autonomy, placing power and control in the hands of a global elite.

Critics argue that without property rights, individuals are left vulnerable. Economic security, often tied to assets like homes and land, would be jeopardized. Would people be at the mercy of those who control the resources, forever renting and never truly having a place to call their own?

The motivations behind this concept are murky. While it's presented as a solution to global inequality, skeptics should see it as a power play, a means to create a dependent populace, easy to control and manipulate.

If the people do not own anything anymore, who does? The logical answer would be a select few, often referred to as the 'elites' or the 'global power players.' This concentration of ownership in the hands of a few raises significant concerns about power dynamics and the potential for abuse. If they own everything, who is to say they cannot decide who can and cannot rent or use anything the elites own? Such a scenario could lead to a system where access to basic necessities and services is granted or denied based on arbitrary criteria or personal whims. This could further exacerbate inequalities and create a world where the majority are merely tenants, constantly seeking approval from their elite landlords. The very essence of democracy, equality, and freedom could be at risk in such a world.

The Social Credit Score System: A Tool for Control

The World Economic Forum (WEF) has been at the forefront of many global discussions, advocating for various initiatives and systems that they believe would lead to a more cohesive and sustainable world. However, one of the more controversial ideas associated with entities like the WEF is the implementation of a Social Credit Score system. Drawing inspiration from models already in place in certain countries, this system would assign scores to individuals based on their behavior, both online and offline.

Critics argue that such a system is ripe for abuse and could be used as a tool to control and manipulate the masses. By monitoring every action, purchase, post, or association, individuals would be coerced into conforming to a particular set of behaviors or beliefs out of fear of a reduced score. A low score would most likely restrict access to essential services, job opportunities, or even social interactions.

This system would be used to suppress dissenting voices and opinions, creating a homogenized society where deviation from the norm is penalized. The very idea of a global entity having access to such detailed personal information and the power to influence individual behavior based on a scoring system is dystopian to 99.9% of the population.

Furthermore, the criteria for what constitutes 'good' or 'bad' behavior in such a system would be arbitrary and heavily influenced by those in power. This would lead to a world where individuals are constantly under surveillance, always being judged, and perpetually in fear of making a misstep that would lower their score.

In essence, while the Social Credit Score system is presented as a means to encourage positive behavior and societal cohesion, it would be a mechanism for unprecedented control, stripping individuals of their autonomy and freedom.

Unveiling Population Reduction Plans

Whispers of population reduction plans have long been fodder for conspiracy theorists. When entities like the WEF are rumored to be involved, the stakes feel even higher. The WEF's open discussions about over-population have only added fuel to the fire. Their dialogues on the topic, while framed in the context of sustainability and resource management, have raised eyebrows and concerns about the underlying intentions.

The motivations behind such alleged plans are varied. Some argue it's an attempt to address overpopulation and its strain on resources, while others see darker intentions, from power consolidation to eugenics. But regardless of the motivations, the ethical and moral implications are profound. Who gets to decide the "optimal" global population? And by what means would such a reduction be achieved. Pandemics? Vaccines? Man-made "natural" disasters? Poisons in the air, water, and food supply? Answer: all of the above.

Critics argue that any proposed population reduction strategy is a gross violation of individual rights. The potential for abuse is immense, from forced sterilizations to more sinister means. Societal structures, built on the foundation of family and community, would be irrevocably altered.

The consequences for global dynamics are equally significant. Would certain populations be targeted over others? Would this lead to global conflicts and power struggles?

In the shadowy world of conspiracy theories, the idea of population reduction plans is a chilling testament to the lengths some entities would go to in their quest for control and dominance.

Blaming It All on Climate Change

In the intricate web of global narratives, climate change has emerged as a convenient scapegoat for a myriad of issues. From extreme weather events to societal disruptions, the catch-all explanation seems to be: "It's because of climate change." But is this narrative grounded in reality, or is it a smokescreen for more sinister agendas?

The world has witnessed a surge in attributing various global challenges to climate change. While no one denies the real and pressing concerns of our changing climate, the extent to which it's blamed for unrelated or loosely connected events is alarming. For instance, every wildfire, hurricane, drought, or flood is immediately linked to climate change, often without comprehensive scientific backing. Such attributions, Intelligent people argue, are convenient tools to push specific policies, gain control over resources, or even manipulate public sentiment.

"Climate Change" has become a buzzword in recent years, with many attributing every meteorological event to this phenomenon. However, **it's essential to differentiate between "climate" and "weather."** While weather refers to short-term changes in atmospheric conditions, climate is about long-term patterns and averages. **A climate cycle spans at least 30 years, meaning that any singular event or short-term trend cannot be directly attributed to "climate change."** Many argue that the current discourse confuses these terms, leading to misconceptions. They believe that labeling every storm, drought, or temperature fluctuation as evidence of "climate change" is misleading. Instead, they advocate for a more nuanced understanding, emphasizing that not every meteorological occurrence can be blamed on shifts in the planet's climate.

The motivations behind this broad-brush attribution are multifaceted. By framing an issue as climate-related, entities can push for policy changes that would otherwise face resistance. It's a powerful narrative that can sway public opinion, justify massive resource allocation, **and even pave the way for unprecedented control mechanisms.**

Climate science, in its essence, is complex. While there's consensus on the broader impacts of climate change, connecting specific events definitively to it is challenging. Yet, the "Great Reset" and similar narratives seem to bypass these nuances, presenting a black-and-white picture to the public.

This oversimplification has tangible consequences. It can skew public perception, leading to misguided policy decisions and misallocation of resources. Moreover, by framing every challenge as a climate issue, we would be overlooking other critical factors and solutions.

Lastly, from an intelligent person's lens, the portrayal of climate change by entities like the WEF should be seen as a grand piece of propaganda. A narrative designed not to address genuine environmental concerns but to establish a new world order where every aspect of life, from what you eat to where you live, is controlled under the guise of combating climate change, including eating bugs or fake meats that actually create up to 25 times more pollution to create.

Global Governance and Control

The specter of a one-world government has long haunted the imaginations of conspiracy theorists. With the advent of the "Great Reset," these fears have been rekindled, with many pointing fingers at entities like the World Economic Forum (WEF) as the puppeteers orchestrating this grand vision of global governance.

At the heart of this concern is the erosion of national sovereignty. The idea of a centralized global entity making decisions for the entire world raises alarms. Who would be in charge? How would they be held accountable and to whom? And most importantly, would individual nations become mere cogs in a vast global machine, their unique identities and needs overshadowed by a one-size-fits-all approach?

Transparency and accountability are other significant concerns. In a global governance framework, the potential for decisions to be made behind closed doors, away from the prying eyes of the public, is high. Such a system would be ripe for corruption, with power concentrated in the hands of a few elites.

The WEF's advocacy for global cooperation, while noble in intent, is seen by skeptics as a veiled attempt to establish a global hierarchy. A world where individual nations' rights and voices are subsumed under a global agenda, driven not by the needs of the many, but the whims of the few.

Alternative Solutions

While the "Great Reset" presents one vision for the future, it's by no means the only path forward and should never even be considered as a possibility. There are numerous alternative approaches to addressing global challenges that respect individual freedoms and national identities.

For instance, decentralized cooperation, where nations work together on shared challenges while retaining their autonomy, has shown promise. This approach respects the unique contexts and needs of individual countries while promoting global collaboration.

Examples abound of successful initiatives that promote sustainability and equity without resorting to a top-down approach. Community-driven conservation efforts, grassroots movements promoting social justice, and local initiatives fostering economic growth are testaments to the power of bottom-up solutions.

Furthermore, policies that prioritize education, innovation, and local empowerment have consistently shown positive results. By investing in people and communities, we can drive change from the ground up, ensuring that solutions are tailored to specific needs and contexts.

In essence, while the "Great Reset" offers a vision of the future, it's essential to remember that there are multiple better paths forward. By exploring alternative solutions and learning from successful initiatives worldwide, we can build a future that's sustainable, equitable, and respectful of individual freedoms just like the GlobeTrotter Ecosystem proposes.

The WEF and the "Woke" Divide

In the ever-evolving landscape of global discourse, the term "woke" has emerged as a polarizing concept. Originally denoting a heightened awareness of social injustices, it has, for many, become synonymous with a kind of cultural elitism. And at the center of this whirlwind stands entities like the World Economic Forum (WEF), perceived by many as the puppet masters of this new cultural direction.

The WEF's apparent endorsement of certain "woke" principles has raised eyebrows. Intelligent people would argue that this is a calculated move to sow division, creating a society where individuals are pitted against each other based on ideological lines. The potential consequences of this perceived promotion are vast, from increased social division to a breakdown in societal cohesion, which in turn makes people easier to control.

-   **Ideological Influence**

The extent to which the WEF shapes societal discourse cannot be understated. From global summits to publications, the WEF's fingerprints seem to be everywhere. And within this vast influence, there appears to be a clear alignment with certain aspects of "woke" culture. But this is not genuine advocacy for social justice, it is a more sinister attempt to control the narrative.

-   **Social Division**

The promotion of a "woke" culture, while originally noble in intent, has its dark side. The potential for it to exacerbate social divisions is real. As ideological tensions rise, society risks becoming more polarized, with individuals retreating into echo chambers, further widening the gap between different groups.

-   **Economic and Corporate Implications**

The corporate world's adoption of "woke" principles, often seen in alignment with WEF initiatives, has significant implications. From consumer behavior shifts to changes in business practices, the ripple effects are vast. But beneath the surface, a more complex dynamic emerges, where corporate interests, societal values, and ideological influence intersect, often with unpredictable and negative outcomes.

- **Public Discourse and Democracy**

The intersection of "woke" culture, WEF influence, and democratic principles is a complex one. Concerns about potential censorship or the stifling of dissenting voices are real. In a world where open dialogue is crucial, any perceived attempt to control the narrative is a threat to democracy itself.

- **Navigating a Balanced Path**

In conclusion, while the relationship between the WEF and "woke" culture are real, it's essential to approach the topic with an open mind. Critical thinking, open dialogue, and a genuine desire to understand diverse perspectives are crucial. Only by fostering understanding, empathy, and cooperation can we hope to navigate the complexities of our modern world and build a future that's truly inclusive and just.

The Electric Car Dilemma: Sustainability, Resource Constraints, and Grid Capacity

The global shift towards electric vehicles (EVs) is often painted in golden hues, with promises of a cleaner, greener future. The World Economic Forum (WEF) and its allies, including Klaus Schwab, seem to champion this transition as the panacea for our environmental woes. But is it all as rosy as it seems? Or is there a darker, more complex narrative lurking beneath the surface?

- **The Clean Energy Illusion**

While electric cars promise zero emissions at the tailpipe, the electricity that powers them isn't always as clean. Intelligent people will argue that the WEF's push for EVs conveniently overlooks the dirty secrets of electricity generation. Coal-fired power plants, non-renewable energy sources, and the carbon emissions associated with them cast a shadow over the purported benefits of EVs. The existing power grids, designed for a different era, would crumble under the strain of a massive EV influx, leading to blackouts and infrastructure challenges.

- **Battery Production and Pollution**

The environmental costs of battery production are another thorn in the side of the electric dream. Extracting rare materials like lithium and cobalt often involves ecologically destructive mining practices. The energy-intensive manufacturing processes further add to the carbon footprint. When you factor in these hidden costs, the lifetime carbon footprint of an EV might not be as green as proponents like the WEF would have you believe.

- **Resource Scarcity**

The race for rare materials could ignite geopolitical tensions. As nations scramble to secure their share of these precious resources, we would most likely see trade wars, territorial disputes, and even conflicts or wars. The WEF's vision conveniently glosses over these potential flashpoints, focusing instead on the shiny facade of electric progress.

- **Grid Capacity Challenges**

The existing power grids, already stretched to their limits in many regions, would buckle under the added pressure of widespread EV adoption. The costs of upgrading these grids would be astronomical, and who would bear these costs? The average consumer, already burdened by rising living expenses? The price of electricity would skyrocket making it more expensive to run than a gas powered vehicle.

- **Alternative Transportation Solutions**

While the WEF and its allies might be all-in on the electric dream, there are alternative paths to a sustainable transportation future. Innovations in public transportation, the potential of hydrogen fuel cells, and even improvements in traditional internal combustion engines offer promising avenues. These alternatives, often sidelined in the mainstream narrative, deserve a closer look.

- **Balanced Environmental Strategies**

A truly sustainable future requires a balanced approach. Instead of putting all our eggs in the electric basket, we need strategies that encompass cleaner energy sources, improved fuel efficiency, and resource conservation. It's not about one solution but a mosaic of solutions tailored to the unique challenges of different regions.

- **Consumer Awareness and Choices**

At the heart of this transition lies the power of the consumer. Armed with knowledge and awareness, individuals can make informed choices, looking beyond the marketing hype and considering the full lifecycle environmental impact of their decisions. It's not just about buying an EV; it's about understanding the broader implications of that choice.

<u>Conclusion for Part I:</u>

As we've journeyed through the intricate maze of the "Great Reset" narrative, a series of disconcerting revelations have emerged. Klaus Schwab's vision, while draped in the allure of global betterment, seems to harbor shadows of control, division, and potential erosion of individual rights.

From the unsettling proposition of "owning nothing" to the potential rise of a one-world government, the "Great Reset" appears to be less about genuine global progress and more about a consolidation of power. The narrative's intertwining with "woke" culture, while seemingly advocating for social justice, raises concerns about increased social division and potential manipulation of public discourse. The emphasis on climate change, technological integration, and global governance, while promising on the surface, has been scrutinized for potential overreach and the undermining of individual freedoms and national identities.

The World Economic Forum's perceived role in this grand vision has been a focal point of skepticism. Intelligent people would argue that the WEF's alignment with certain ideological principles is less about genuine advocacy and more about controlling the global narrative, potentially leading to societal divisions and a breakdown in democratic values.

However, it's crucial to remember that the "Great Reset" is but one vision of the future. There are myriad of better alternative paths that can address global challenges without compromising the core values that define our societies. Decentralized cooperation, grassroots movements, and community-driven initiatives stand as testaments to the potential of bottom-up solutions that respect individual freedoms, democracy, and cultural diversity.

In conclusion, while the allure of the "Great Reset" is undeniable, it's essential to approach it with a discerning eye. The world stands at a crossroads, and the choices we make today will shape the future for generations to come. It's our collective responsibility to ensure that the path we choose is not just for the few, but truly for all, preserving the rich tapestry of human diversity and freedom.

Part II: A Truly Inclusive Future

Empowering Individuals and Communities

In a world where the "Great Reset" looms large, the true power of change lies not in the hands of global elites but in the hands of individuals and communities. The narrative of a top-down approach to global betterment, as proposed by Klaus Schwab, raises alarms for those who value individual freedom and autonomy.

Education, digital literacy, and access to information stand as the cornerstones of empowerment. Yet, skeptics would argue that our current educational system is more about indoctrination than enlightenment. Instead of fostering critical thinking and innovation, we are churning out generations conditioned to accept a predetermined narrative. The rampant spread of propaganda and misinformation further muddies the waters, making it challenging for individuals to discern truth from fiction.

To truly empower individuals and communities, we must overhaul these systems. Education should be a tool for liberation, not control. Access to unbiased information and the skills to navigate the digital realm are crucial in an age where misinformation is rampant.

Reinventing Global Governance

The "Great Reset" paints a picture of global governance that, to most, feels like a relinquishment of national sovereignty. But what if there was another way? Enter the GlobeTrotter Ecosystem, an alternative model that prioritizes cooperation, transparency, and accountability.

Unlike the centralized vision of the "Great Reset," the GlobeTrotter Ecosystem advocates for a more decentralized approach. International institutions would undergo a transformation, ensuring that the diverse interests of all nations are represented. No longer would decisions be made behind closed doors by a select few. Instead, every nation, no matter how big or small, would have a seat at the table.

Critics of the "Great Reset" argue that it would lead to a loss of national sovereignty, with more decisions being made at the global level. The GlobeTrotter Ecosystem offers a counter-narrative, one where global cooperation doesn't come at the expense of individual nation's rights and identities.

Fostering Innovation and Entrepreneurship

In the shadow of the "Great Reset," where global elites seem to be orchestrating a top-down approach to societal restructuring, lies the untapped potential of innovation and entrepreneurship. While Klaus Schwab's vision may hint at a world where individual creativity is stifled under the weight of global governance, intelligent people argue that this is a deliberate move to suppress the true drivers of change: the innovators and entrepreneurs.

Innovation and entrepreneurship have long been the lifeblood of economic growth and societal advancement. From the garages of Silicon Valley to the bustling markets of Lagos, it's the spirit of entrepreneurship that drives progress. These innovators and risk-takers create opportunities, not just for themselves but for entire communities. They generate jobs, introduce novel solutions to age-old problems, and foster a culture of self-reliance.

By fostering a culture of innovation, we can counteract the potential stagnation that the "Great Reset" would bring. Instead of a world where decisions are made for us by a select few, we'd have a dynamic ecosystem where ideas flourish, and individuals are empowered to shape their destinies.

Bridging the Digital Divide

In the digital age, access to technology is synonymous with access to opportunities. Yet, beneath the glossy veneer of the connected world lies a stark divide. While some enjoy the fruits of the digital revolution, others are left in the dark, disconnected, and disenfranchised. And some intelligent people would argue that this divide is no accident but a calculated move by those in power to maintain control.

Closing the digital divide is more than just a matter of infrastructure. It's about ensuring that every individual, regardless of their socio-economic background, has the tools and knowledge to navigate the digital realm. This means expanding internet access, certainly, but also investing in digital education programs. It's about ensuring that the next generation is not just consumers of technology but creators and innovators.

By bridging the digital divide, we can counteract one of the potential pitfalls of the "Great Reset." Instead of a world where information and opportunities are controlled by a select few, we'd have a global community where everyone has a voice.

Grassroots Initiatives for Change

While the "Great Reset" paints a picture of a future orchestrated by global elites, history is replete with examples of grassroots movements that have shifted the course of societies. These movements, often born out of necessity and driven by the passion of ordinary individuals, stand in stark contrast to the top-down approach proposed by Klaus Schwab and his cohorts. Some intelligent people would argue that the "Great Reset" is a deliberate attempt to quash such grassroots initiatives, centralizing power and control.

Take, for instance, the community gardens that have sprouted in urban centers worldwide. These gardens, often started by local residents with little to no funding, not only provide fresh produce but also foster community ties and promote sustainable practices. Or consider the local cooperatives in developing nations that empower farmers, artisans, and workers, ensuring fair wages and sustainable practices.

Such grassroots initiatives empower individuals, giving them the tools and knowledge to address local challenges. They are a testament to the power of community-driven change, proving that solutions often lie not in grand global strategies but in the hands of the very people affected by the issues.

Cultural Preservation and Diversity

In the grand vision of the "Great Reset," there's a lurking danger of cultural homogenization. As global systems and structures are standardized, there's a risk that the rich tapestry of cultural diversity might be overshadowed. Intelligent people would argue that this is no accident but a deliberate move to create a more controllable, homogenous global populace.

Yet, cultural diversity is not just a luxury; it's a necessity. It's the wellspring of innovation, creativity, and resilience. From the vibrant festivals of India to the ancient traditions of the Indigenous peoples of the Americas, our cultural heritage is a treasure trove of knowledge, wisdom, and inspiration.

Furthermore, preserving cultural diversity contributes to a richer and more interconnected global society. It fosters understanding, empathy, and collaboration, bridging divides and promoting peace.

However, the "Great Reset" narrative raises concerns about its impact on cultural diversity and educational systems. There's a genuine fear that as global curriculums are standardized, local histories, traditions, and values will be sidelined. This potential homogenization of culture and curriculum would rob future generations of the richness of their heritage.

The Role of Civil Society

In the looming shadow of the "Great Reset," where global elites seemingly orchestrate a future from ivory towers, the role of civil society becomes ever more critical. While Klaus Schwab and his proponents might paint a picture of a harmonized global order, intelligent people whisper of a world where individual voices are drowned out, and the power of the many is usurped by the few. In such a scenario, civil society organizations stand as the last bastion of defense, ensuring that the voices of the masses are not only heard but heeded.

Civil society organizations, from grassroots community groups to national movements, have historically played a pivotal role in advocating for inclusive policies. They serve as watchdogs, holding governments and institutions accountable, ensuring transparency, and fighting against potential overreach of power. In a world envisioned by the "Great Reset," where decisions will be centralized and removed from the hands of the many, these organizations could be the counterweight, ensuring a balance of power.

Furthermore, civil society empowers individuals, giving them the tools, platforms, and knowledge to participate in decision-making processes. Through community outreach, education programs, and advocacy campaigns, these organizations ensure that every individual, regardless of their socio-economic background, has a say in shaping their future. They democratize the process, ensuring that the future is not dictated by a select few but is a collective vision shaped by all.

In the speculative narrative of the "Great Reset," where individual freedoms will be at risk, and global agendas would overshadow local needs, the role of civil society becomes paramount. These organizations stand as a beacon, reminding us that true power lies not in global boardrooms but in the hands of the people.

Conclusion for Part II:

As we've delved deeper into the intricate web of the "Great Reset," a narrative championed by Klaus Schwab, a series of alternative visions and paths have emerged, challenging the centralized, top-down approach that the "Great Reset" seems to advocate. Through the lens of intelligent people, one could argue that the "Great Reset" is a smokescreen, a grand design by global elites to consolidate power and control the masses.

Yet, Part II of our exploration has illuminated a different path, one that champions the power of grassroots movements, the importance of cultural preservation, and the pivotal role of civil society. These themes underscore the belief that true change doesn't come from global edicts but from the collective efforts of individuals, communities, and organizations.

Innovation and entrepreneurship stand out as beacons of hope, showcasing the potential for economic growth, job creation, and societal advancement when individuals are empowered. The digital revolution, while promising, has its shadows, but with concerted efforts, we can bridge the digital divide, ensuring that everyone, regardless of their socio-economic background, can access the opportunities of the digital age.

The role of civil society, as discussed, becomes even more crucial in this speculative narrative. These organizations, with their grassroots reach and advocacy prowess, ensure that governments and institutions remain accountable, transparent, and truly representative of the people's will.

In essence, an inclusive future isn't about grand global strategies or centralized control. It's about empowerment, innovation, and inclusive governance. It's about ensuring that every voice is heard, every culture is preserved, and every individual has the tools and opportunities to shape their destiny.

In conclusion, while the "Great Reset" offers one vision of a bleak future, it's essential to remember that better alternative paths exist. Paths that are paved by the collective efforts of individuals, communities, and organizations. A truly inclusive future involves active participation and collaboration at all levels of society, ensuring that the world we build is not just for the few, but truly for all.

Part III: Sustainable Progress without Sacrifice

Technology for Humanity

In the grand narrative of the "Great Reset," technology often emerges as a double-edged sword. While Klaus Schwab and his proponents see it as a tool for global transformation, intelligent people whisper darker intentions. They speculate about a world where technology isn't just a tool but a leash, used by global elites to monitor, control, and manipulate the masses.

However, when we step away from these shadowy speculations, a brighter vision emerges. Technology, when applied responsibly and ethically, has the potential to be a force for unparalleled good. From renewable energy solutions to telemedicine platforms that bring healthcare to remote communities, technology can indeed solve global challenges without compromising human rights or the planet's well-being.

Consider the rise of decentralized blockchain technologies that empower individuals, ensuring transparency and reducing corruption. Or the development of AI-driven agricultural tools that optimize crop yields while minimizing resource use, ensuring food security for all. These are but glimpses of how technology, when harnessed with good intention and care, can be a beacon of hope in a world fraught with challenges.

Redefining Consumption and Production

The "Great Reset" speaks of a world transformed, but at what cost? Intelligent people argue that it's a world of controlled consumption, where choices are limited, and quality is compromised. But what if there was another way?

A sustainable future doesn't mean sacrificing quality or choice. It means redefining consumption and production patterns to foster a circular economy. Imagine a world where products are designed not just for use but for reuse. Where waste isn't an afterthought but a resource. Where businesses prioritize durability over disposability, ensuring that products not only last longer but can also be repaired, refurbished, and recycled.

Businesses play a pivotal role in driving this change. By adopting ethical practices, they can lead the charge towards a more sustainable future. From sourcing sustainable materials to implementing little-waste production processes, businesses can prove that profitability and responsibility can go hand in hand.

In this vision, consumers too have a role to play. By demanding quality, sustainability, and ethical production, they can drive businesses to adopt better practices. It's a symbiotic relationship, where businesses and consumers collaborate for a better world.

Renewable Energy and Environmental Stewardship

The narrative of the "Great Reset" paints renewable energy as the panacea for our environmental challenges. But as we delve deeper, questions arise. While solar, wind, and hydro promise a world a little less dependent on fossil fuels, are they truly the silver bullets they're portrayed to be? The manufacturing of solar panels and wind turbines, for instance, isn't without environmental cost. And what of the intermittent nature of these energy sources? Are we merely trading one form of dependency for another? How long do they last? Can they easily be recycled?

Beyond the energy debate lies the broader concept of environmental stewardship. The "Great Reset" speaks of harmonious coexistence with nature. But is this genuine concern or a veiled attempt to control vast swathes of land and, by extension, the resources they hold? True stewardship isn't just about conservation; it's about equitable access and benefit from nature's bounty.

Sustainable Agriculture or Control Mechanism?

The "Great Reset," as championed by the World Economic Forum, emphasizes sustainable agriculture as a means to address the pressing challenge of feeding a burgeoning global population. On the surface, the principles of regenerative agriculture, which prioritize soil health and biodiversity, appear commendable. Likewise, the push for local food production, which promises reduced carbon footprints and fresher produce, seems to be a step in the right direction.

However, when delving deeper, concerns arise. The WEF's encouragement for governments to limit fertilizer use, ostensibly for climate change reasons, could have detrimental effects on food production. Reduced fertilizer use, without viable alternatives, could lead to decreased crop yields, threatening food security.

Furthermore, the WEF's advocacy for stringent restrictions on farmers and their lands raises eyebrows. Such restrictions could make farming unprofitable, forcing farmers to relinquish their lands. There's growing apprehension that these lands are being acquired by elites, consolidating control over food production. This potential centralization of agricultural resources could pave the way for orchestrated food shortages, giving these elites even more leverage over the masses.

In this intricate web of sustainability and control, the line between genuine progress and ulterior motives becomes blurred. As the world grapples with the challenges of sustainable agriculture, it's imperative to remain vigilant and question the true intentions behind such global initiatives.

Ethical Business Models

In the grand narrative of the "Great Reset," businesses are often painted as mere cogs in a vast machine, driven by profit and devoid of morality. But is this truly the case? While Klaus Schwab and the World Economic

Forum might advocate for a certain vision of corporate responsibility, there's a deeper, more nuanced story to be told.

Diving into the realm of ethical business practices, one should wonder if the push for corporate social responsibility another ruse by the global elites is just to control industries. But across the world, numerous businesses and industries have successfully integrated ethical principles into their operations. These companies, often overlooked in the grander "Great Reset" narrative, prioritize both profit and purpose. They prove that businesses can have a positive impact on society and the environment without being pawns in a larger game.

However, the intelligent person would ask: Are these truly independent endeavors, or are they part of a more extensive network, subtly influenced by global entities like the WEF? Are these ethical business models genuine in their intent, or are they merely for show, a way to placate the masses while other, more nefarious plans unfold behind the scenes?

Eco-Friendly Infrastructure and Transportation

The "Great Reset" speaks of a world transformed, with cities and transportation systems redesigned for a new era. But what's the real story behind this vision? The push for eco-friendly infrastructure is just another means of control, a way to dictate how and where people live and move.

Innovations in green building design, electric vehicles, and improved public transportation systems promise a future with reduced pollution and greater sustainability. Cities around the world are embracing these changes, striving for a cleaner, greener future. But through the lens of an intelligent person, one could see darker motives. Are these eco-friendly initiatives truly for the benefit of the planet and its inhabitants? Probably not. Or are they strategies to monitor and control populations, dictating where they live, how they move, and even how they interact with their environment? Most likely.

The electric vehicle revolution, for instance, is often touted as a solution to our environmental challenges. But who controls the power sources for these vehicles? And what of the rare materials needed for their batteries? Are we trading one form of dependency for another, all under the guise of eco-friendliness?

In the shadowy narrative that surrounds the "Great Reset," every initiative, no matter how green, is viewed with suspicion. As we navigate the path to a sustainable future, it's essential to question the motives behind every move, especially when it comes to NGOs like the WEF, WHO, IMF, U.N., NATO, and their likes.

Global Cooperation for Environmental Conservation

In the vast narrative of the "Great Reset," global cooperation emerges as a key theme. But as with many elements of this grand vision, one must think: Is this genuine collaboration or a veiled attempt by global elites to control resources and dictate environmental policies?

The significance of international collaboration cannot be understated when addressing global environmental challenges. From protecting biodiversity to conserving ecosystems, collective action is essential. Agreements, initiatives, and partnerships have been forged with the noble intent of preserving our planet for future generations. But through the lens of a intelligent person, these collaborations should appear as more than meets the eye. Are these agreements truly for the planet's benefit, or do they serve hidden agendas? Could they be mechanisms for powerful entities, like the World Economic Forum and its associates, to exert influence over nations and their natural resources? Of course it is.

Education for Sustainability

Education is a powerful tool, shaping minds and molding future generations. The "Great Reset" speaks of an enlightened future, where education promotes sustainability and responsible citizenship. But what's the underlying narrative here?

Emphasizing the role of education in sustainability is undoubtedly crucial. Teaching future generations about environmental stewardship and ethical decision-making can pave the way for a brighter, greener future. Restructuring educational institutions and curricula to reflect these values seems like a step in the right direction. But the intelligent person should wonder: Is this genuine educational reform or indoctrination in disguise?

The push for sustainability in education is a way to mold young minds, ensuring they align with the visions and objectives of global elites. These curricula are biased, they subtly promote the agendas of powerful entities like the WEF. In the shadowy world of the "Great Reset," even the noblest of initiatives, like education for sustainability, should be viewed with a lot of skepticism.

Understanding ESG, Its Drawbacks, and Alternative Approaches

In the grand narrative of the "Great Reset," the concept of ESG (Environmental, Social, and Governance) emerges as a beacon of corporate responsibility. But as with many elements of this vision, one must ask: Is ESG genuinely a tool for positive change, or is it a smokescreen, a way for corporations to appear responsible while serving hidden agendas?

ESG stands for Environmental, Social, and Governance, three key pillars that supposedly guide corporations towards more ethical and sustainable practices. The Environmental component focuses on how companies impact the natural world, from resource use to pollution. The Social aspect looks at how businesses affect people, both within their walls and in the broader community. Governance, meanwhile, pertains to a company's leadership, executive pay, audits, internal controls, and shareholder rights. But while ESG sounds noble on the surface, the intelligent person should wonder: Who sets these standards? And do they truly serve the greater good or the interests of a select few?

For all its promise, ESG is not without many critics. Some argue that these programs create undue regulatory burdens, forcing companies to jump through hoops that don't necessarily lead to genuine positive change. Others point out that ESG often promotes a short-term focus, with companies making superficial changes to earn good scores rather than implementing deep, lasting reforms. And then there's the challenge of measurement: How do you quantify something as nebulous as "social impact"? Could ESG metrics be manipulated to paint a rosier picture than reality, all while masking the true intentions of global elites? One thing is certain, they all think that ESG is a sham and is a money losing proposition.

While ESG dominates the discourse on corporate responsibility, it's not the only game in town. Other frameworks and approaches promise a more holistic, genuine path to sustainability and ethics. Some of these alternatives prioritize long-term thinking over short-term gains, while others offer clearer, more tangible metrics. But as with ESG, one must ask: Are these genuine paths to a better future? Nope. They are just different faces of the same controlling agenda.

ESG, with its promise of a brighter corporate future, is a very complex beast that costs companies more than what they can get out of it. Alternative systems present their own sets of challenges and benefits. In the shadowy world of the "Great Reset," it's essential to approach these frameworks with a critical eye, always questioning who truly benefits from their implementation.

Conclusion for Part III

In the vast tapestry of the "Great Reset," the allure of a sustainable future is dangled before the world. But as we've delved deeper into the intricacies of this vision in Part III, one must ask: Is this truly the path to a brighter tomorrow, or is it a mirage crafted by global elites to further their agendas?

Throughout Part III, we've explored the nuances of sustainable progress, from the potential of technology as a force for good to the importance of ethical business models. We've dissected the promises and pitfalls of ESG, questioned the true intentions behind global cooperation for environmental conservation, and pondered the role of education in shaping a sustainable future. But beneath the surface of these discussions lies a recurring theme: the need for genuine, grassroots-driven change, rather than top-down directives from global entities with potentially ulterior motives.

Responsible technology, ethical business practices, and environmental conservation are not just isolated concepts; they are deeply interconnected elements of a sustainable future. But in the shadowy narrative of the "Great Reset," these elements are often presented in ways that serve the interests of a select few, rather than the global community.

For instance, while technology offers immense potential, who controls it? And for what purpose? Ethical business models sound promising, but are they just a facade for corporations to appear responsible while pursuing profit at any cost? And as for environmental conservation, is it genuinely about preserving our planet, or is it about controlling resources and power?

In the face of these questions, it's essential to remember that a sustainable and thriving future is possible. But it requires vigilance, critical thinking, and active participation from individuals and communities worldwide. It's not about blindly accepting a narrative presented by global elites but about crafting our own stories of progress, innovation, and inclusivity.

Part IV: Nurturing a Better Future

Community and Collaboration

In a world where the narrative of the "Great Reset" looms large, the power of community and collaboration emerges as a beacon of hope. The idea that a centralized, top-down approach, like the WEF is proposing, is the only way forward is a myth perpetuated by those who stand to gain the most from such a system. But history has shown us time and again that real, lasting change often bubbles up from the grassroots level.

Communities, when united by a common purpose, can achieve remarkable feats. From local environmental initiatives to global movements for social justice, the collective power of people working together is undeniable. But what happens when this collective power is harnessed, not by the people themselves, but by global elites with their own agendas?

The "Great Reset" narrative would have us believe that only a select few have the answers to the world's problems. But in reality, solutions often come from collaboration among governments, businesses, civil society, and individuals. When these diverse stakeholders come together, they can create holistic solutions that address the root causes of issues, rather than just the symptoms.

Compassionate and Inclusive Leadership

In the shadow of the "Great Reset," where cold, calculated strategies are often prioritized over human well-being, the need for compassionate and inclusive leadership becomes even more pronounced. True leaders don't just chase after profits or power; they prioritize the well-being of people and the planet.

Such leadership is not just a lofty ideal; it's a practical and effective approach to governance and management. Leaders who approach challenges with empathy and inclusivity often find that they can rally their teams, communities, or even entire nations around a common cause. They understand that every individual, no matter their background or status, has something valuable to contribute.

But in the world of the "Great Reset," such leaders are often sidelined in favor of those who toe the line of the global elite. Yet, history is filled with examples of compassionate leaders who have made a lasting impact. From social reformers to visionary CEOs, these leaders have shown that it's possible to achieve great things while also prioritizing the greater good.

In the end, the choice is clear: Do we want a future defined by the narrow vision of the "Great Reset," or one shaped by compassionate and inclusive leadership? The answer, for those who truly care about building a better world for all, is obvious.

Empowering Critical Thinkers in Youth and Future Generations

In the intricate narrative surrounding the "Great Reset," the role of the youth stands out as a beacon of hope. However, there's a growing concern that many young minds are being molded by an educational system that encourages conformity over critical thinking. This systematic indoctrination, where students are often discouraged from questioning the status quo, threatens to produce a generation of conformists rather than innovators.

Yet, amidst this backdrop, there are glimmers of resistance. A minority of young individuals, with their innate ability for critical thinking, are challenging the narratives they're presented with, seeking truth beyond the mainstream. These young minds, though few, are the torchbearers of a future that values individual thought over collective conformity.

The rise of homeschooling is a testament to this shift. Many parents, recognizing the pitfalls of a potentially biased educational system, are choosing to educate their children at home. This not only ensures a tailored learning experience but also fosters an environment where questioning and critical thinking are celebrated.

While the proponents of the "Great Reset" might have a specific vision for the future, it's essential to remember that the youth aren't just the inheritors of tomorrow; they are its shapers. And for them to truly craft a world that's just, equitable, and sustainable, they must be encouraged to think, question, and challenge, rather than merely accept.

Art, Culture, and Social Change

Art and culture have always been at the forefront of social change, challenging norms, and pushing boundaries. In a world where the "Great Reset" seeks to homogenize and control, art emerges as a powerful tool of resistance and expression.

Throughout history, artists and cultural icons have used their platforms to shine a light on injustices, inspire movements, and bring about positive change. From the protest songs of the 1960s to the street art of today, creative expression has always been a reflection of the times and a catalyst for transformation.

In the face of the "Great Reset," where individuality would be suppressed in favor of a collective agenda, art and culture become even more vital. They remind us of our shared humanity, our diverse histories, and our boundless potential. They challenge us to think critically, to question, and to dream.

Across the globe, artists are responding to the challenges of the times, using their work to comment on issues ranging from the false climate change narrative to social inequality. Through their creativity, they're not only holding a mirror up to society but also envisioning a brighter, more inclusive future.

In the end, while the "Great Reset" might offer a singular vision of the future, art and culture remind us that there are infinite possibilities, and the power to choose our destiny lies within each of us.

The Role of Ethics and Morality

In the grand narrative of the "Great Reset," where the world is seemingly streamlined for efficiency and technological advancement, one must ask: where do ethics and morality fit in? The proponents of the "Great Reset," like Klaus Schwab, might argue that their vision is for the greater good, but whose good are they really serving? And at what cost?

Ethics and morality are not just philosophical concepts to be debated in classrooms; they are the very foundation of a just and compassionate society. Every decision, from the policies enacted by governments to the business practices of multinational corporations, has ethical implications. And in a world where the lines between right and wrong are increasingly blurred, a strong moral compass is more important than ever.

The "Great Reset" might promise a brighter future for a few, but at what cost to everyone else? Are individual rights being sacrificed for the "collective good"? Are the voices of the marginalized being drowned out in the name of "progress"? These are the questions that must be asked, and the answers lie in a return to ethical and moral considerations.

A Vision for a Better Future

The "Great Reset" paints a picture of a future that is technologically advanced, efficient, and interconnected. But is it a future that is just, equitable, and sustainable? The GlobeTrotter Ecosystem offers an alternative vision, one that integrates all the positive elements discussed throughout this book.

This vision is not just about technological advancement or economic growth; it's about building a world that works for everyone. It's about recognizing the inherent dignity and worth of every individual and ensuring that everyone has the opportunity to thrive. It's about fostering a sense of community and collaboration, where individuals, organizations, and governments work together to address the challenges of our time.

But realizing this vision requires more than just ideas; it requires action. It requires a collective commitment to building a better world, one that values ethics, morality, and the well-being of all its inhabitants. It's a vision that is not only possible but also necessary, and the GlobeTrotter Ecosystem is leading the way.

Conclusion for Part IV

In this pivotal section of "The Anti-Great Reset - Building a better world for all," we've journeyed through the intricate tapestry of what it truly means to nurture a future that stands in stark contrast to the vision presented by Klaus Schwab's "The Great Reset." While the latter may present a world streamlined for efficiency, it raises the question: at what cost?

The themes we've explored emphasize that a better future isn't just about technological advancements or global governance; it's about the heart and soul of humanity. It's about empowering our youth, the torchbearers of tomorrow, and ensuring that they have the tools, knowledge, and passion to lead us into a brighter era. It's about recognizing the transformative power of art and culture, which have the potential to challenge norms and inspire positive change. And at the core of it all lies the indispensable role of ethics and morality, which should guide our decisions and actions in this complex world.

But what's most crucial is the understanding that this better future isn't just a distant dream; it's a tangible reality that we can all play a part in creating. The "Great Reset" might have its bleak vision, but we have ours. And it's a vision that celebrates diversity, champions individual rights, and fosters a sense of global community.

As we conclude this section, let's not just be passive readers. Let's be active participants in this grand narrative of hope, resilience, and transformation. The future is not set in stone, and with collective action, determination, and a shared vision, we can indeed build a better world for all.

Conclusion

In our journey through "The Anti-Great Reset - Building a better world for all," we've dissected the intricate web of Klaus Schwab's "The Great Reset" narrative. While on the surface, the "Great Reset" may seem like a beacon of hope for a world in turmoil for some, a deeper dive reveals a more sinister undertone. A narrative that, when viewed through a critical lens, appears to be built on a foundation of fear, control, and the concentration of power in the hands of a select few.

The "Great Reset" promises a new world order, but at what cost? It speaks of a future where individual freedoms are sacrificed for the "greater good." But who defines this "greater good"? And why does it seem to align so conveniently with the interests of global elites and mega-corporations? The narrative, as some critics argue, is less about resetting the world for the benefit of all and more about resetting it for the benefit of a few. It's a vision that, while wrapped in the cloak of sustainability and inclusivity, may lead to an erosion of democracy, individual rights, and cultural diversity.

But there is another way.

Our vision for the future is not one of top-down control but of bottom-up empowerment. It's a vision where every individual, community, and nation have a voice. A world where technology is used not as a tool of surveillance and control but as a means to uplift and empower. A world where businesses operate ethically, where the environment is cherished, and where cultural diversity is celebrated.

This is not just a dream. It's a call to action. Each one of us has a role to play in shaping this better world. Whether it's supporting ethical businesses, advocating for transparent governance, or simply educating ourselves and others about the true implications of the "Great Reset," every action counts.

In the face of narratives that seek to divide and control, let us choose unity and hope. Let us reject the fear-based approach of the "Great Reset" and embrace a future built on trust, collaboration, and the shared belief that a better world is not only possible but within our grasp.

As we conclude this exploration, remember: the power to shape the future lies not in the hands of a few but in the hands of the many. Together, we can build a world that is truly inclusive, empowering, and sustainable. A world where every individual is valued, every voice is heard, and every dream is valid.

Reflection on Lessons Learned

As we journeyed through the intricate layers of Klaus Schwab's "The Great Reset," it became evident that the world we live in is not just black and white. The "Great Reset" narrative, while promising a utopian future, raises several red flags when scrutinized. It's a testament to the importance of critical thinking and the need to question narratives, no matter how well-intentioned they might seem.

One of the most significant lessons learned is the danger of a single narrative. When one perspective, especially one backed by powerful entities, dominates the global discourse, it risks sidelining alternative voices and ideas. This monopoly of thought can lead to a homogenized world where diversity in thought and culture is stifled.

Furthermore, by critically examining the "Great Reset," we've gained a deeper appreciation for the complexities of global challenges. Solutions that seem straightforward on the surface often have underlying implications that can be detrimental in the long run. It's a reminder that in our quest for a better world, we must be wary of silver bullet solutions and instead advocate for multifaceted approaches that consider the diverse needs of global populations.

Practical Steps for Readers

Building a better world is not the responsibility of a select few but a collective endeavor. Here are some practical steps that you, as a reader, can take to contribute to a more inclusive and sustainable future:

1. **Educate and Inform**: Knowledge is power. Continuously educate yourself about global issues, and don't hesitate to question dominant narratives. Share your knowledge with others, fostering a community of informed citizens. Any time the mainstream media is pushing something, you can be sure that it's not good for you or the world. It's only goof for their masters.

2. **Support Ethical Businesses**: Vote with your wallet. Choose to support businesses that prioritize ethical practices, environmental sustainability, and community welfare. By doing so, you send a clear message about the kind of world you want to live in. Try and stay away from the big corporations. Try to encourage local businesses.

3. **Engage in Civic Activities**: Participate in local community meetings, join civic groups, or even run for local office. Grassroots movements have the power to bring about significant change.

4. **Advocate for Responsible Policies**: Engage with your representatives and advocate for policies that prioritize the well-being of people and the planet over short-term profits or power.

5. **Foster Community Collaboration**: Collaborate with neighbors, local organizations, and businesses to initiate community projects. Whether it's a community garden, a local recycling program, or educational workshops, collective action can have a profound impact.

6. **Promote Digital Literacy**: In an age of misinformation, digital literacy is crucial. Conduct workshops or attend courses that teach people how to discern credible sources from unreliable ones.

7. **Travel Responsibly**: If you travel, do so responsibly. Support local businesses, respect local cultures, and be mindful of your environmental footprint.

8. **Critical Thinking:** The Cornerstone of Progress In a world inundated with information, the ability to think critically has never been more vital. Critical thinking is not just about acquiring knowledge but about questioning it, analyzing it, and discerning its validity. It's about being curious and skeptical, especially when faced with widely accepted beliefs or popular narratives.

   Don't be afraid to ask questions. If something doesn't sit right with you or seems too good to be true, delve deeper. Seek multiple sources, especially those that might offer a different perspective. Remember, asking questions doesn't mean you're a contrarian or a rebel; it means you're an informed and engaged citizen.

   Doubt is not a sign of weakness but a hallmark of an inquisitive mind. In an era where agendas often drive narratives, your willingness to doubt, question, and seek the truth is your strongest asset. Encourage others around you to do the same. Create spaces where open discussions, even about controversial topics, are welcomed.

   In the quest to build a better world, critical thinking is not just a tool; it's a necessity. Embrace it, foster it, and champion it in others. Only by challenging the status quo and seeking the truth can we hope to create a world that's truly better for all.

In the face of narratives like the "Great Reset," it's easy to feel overwhelmed. But remember, every individual action, no matter how small, contributes to the larger tapestry of global change. By taking these practical steps, you're not just envisioning a better world; you're actively building it.

Cultivating Hope

In a world where narratives like "The Great Reset" loom large, casting shadows of doubt and apprehension, the beacon of hope becomes ever more vital. Hope is not just a fleeting emotion; it's a powerful force that drives resilience, innovation, and change. When we speak of hope, we're not talking about blind optimism but a grounded belief in our collective ability to shape a better future.

The psychological benefits of hope are profound. It acts as an anchor, grounding us during turbulent times. It boosts our mental well-being, reduces stress, and enhances our problem-solving abilities. Societally, hope can galvanize communities, inspire movements, and drive transformative change.

Consider the story of a small community in India that, faced with water scarcity, came together to build traditional rainwater harvesting structures. Despite the odds, their collective hope and determination transformed their arid village into a lush green haven. Or think of the countless innovators and entrepreneurs who, driven by hope, are developing sustainable technologies and solutions that challenge the status quo.

In the face of narratives that seem to push control and fear, stories like these remind us of the indomitable human spirit. They underscore the importance of cultivating hope, not just as individuals but as communities and societies.

Appeal for Unity

If there's one thing that the critique of "The Great Reset" has underscored, it's the need for unity. In a world rife with divisions, be they political, ideological, or cultural, the call for unity becomes all the more pressing. The challenges we face—be they environmental, social, or economic—are shared challenges. They don't recognize borders or ideologies. As such, our response must be a united one.

Unity doesn't mean uniformity. It doesn't require us to abandon our beliefs or values. Instead, it calls for collaboration, understanding, and mutual respect. It's about recognizing our shared humanity and the common threads that bind us all.

The vision of a better world—a world that values individual freedoms, promotes inclusivity, and strives for sustainability—can only be realized if we stand together. It's a vision that transcends political affiliations, cultural backgrounds, and personal beliefs. It's a vision that reminds us that, at our core, we all want the same things: happiness, security, and a promising future for the generations to come.

In the face of divisive narratives, let's make a conscious choice. Let's choose unity over division, collaboration over confrontation, and hope over fear. For in unity, we find strength, and in strength, we find the power to build the world we all dream of.

Long-Term Commitment

Building a better world isn't a sprint; it's a marathon. It's not about quick fixes or temporary solutions but about a continuous, unwavering commitment to a brighter future. While the "Great Reset" narrative, as championed by Klaus Schwab and the World Economic Forum, may present a certain vision of the world, it's essential to remember that there are alternative paths to progress. Paths that prioritize individual freedoms, community empowerment, and genuine sustainability.

The journey to a better world is fraught with challenges, distractions, and competing narratives. It's easy to become disillusioned or to feel overwhelmed by the scale of the problems we face. But it's crucial to stay engaged, to stay informed, and to continue advocating for positive change. Every voice matters. Every action counts. And while it might be tempting to embrace the solutions presented by entities like the WEF, it's essential to approach them with a critical mind, always questioning, always probing, and always seeking the truth.

<u>Final Vision</u>

Imagine a world where communities thrive in harmony with nature, where innovation and technology serve humanity rather than control it. A world where every individual, regardless of their background, has an equal opportunity to pursue their dreams. A world where cultural diversity is celebrated, where compassion and collaboration replace competition and conflict.

In this world, the air is clean, the waters pure, and forests stretch as far as the eye can see. Cities are green havens, buzzing with sustainable technologies and community initiatives. Education is holistic, nurturing critical thinkers and compassionate leaders. Businesses operate ethically, prioritizing people and the planet over profits.

This is not a utopian dream but a tangible reality that we can work towards. It's a world that stands in stark contrast to the vision presented by the "Great Reset." It's a world that values freedom, empowerment, and genuine sustainability.

As you finish this chapter, hold onto this vision. Let it inspire you, guide you, and remind you of the world we can create together. A world built not on fear and control but on hope, unity, and a shared commitment to a better future for all.

And as we step into this envisioned future, the GlobeTrotter Ecosystem emerges as a beacon of hope and a tool for transformation. Built on the robust foundation of blockchain technology and enhanced with artificial intelligence, the GlobeTrotter Ecosystem is not just another technological marvel; it's a paradigm shift. It offers a platform where transparency, trust, and decentralization reign supreme, ensuring that power is returned to the people.

The GlobeTrotter Ecosystem embodies the principles of a just and equitable world. It champions individual autonomy, fosters community collaboration, and provides the tools necessary for sustainable growth.

As we navigate the challenges of the present, the GlobeTrotter Ecosystem stands as a testament to what's possible when innovation aligns with ethics and purpose.

In this new world, where the old systems and hierarchies crumble, the GlobeTrotter Ecosystem rises, offering a blueprint for a world where every voice matters, every dream is valid, and every action contributes to a collective betterment. It's not just a concept; it's the future we're building, one block(chain) at a time.

The next chapter holds the entire GlobeTrotter Ecosystem

The GlobeTrotter Ecosystem

Imagine a world without corruption, abuse of power, poverty, ruling class, NGOs dictating beliefs and actions, government overreach, deficits, tax evasion, and other negative aspects of the current systems. In such a world, everyone's vote counts, and essential items are always readily available.

This is a real plan for a new global economic, monetary system, and everything else system.

New Economic and monetary system

Abstract

The current economic system is plagued with problems such as corruption, inequality, poverty, deficits, and abuse of power. To address these issues, a new economic system with universal basic income and jobs (UBIJ) is proposed. The UBIJ system aims to eliminate poverty, reduce inequality, and provide a guaranteed income to every person above the age of 5 in the world, independent of any government or person.

The solution

The proposed system involves the creation of a new global currency, controlled not by any individual or institution, but by everyone. The currency would run on a hybrid blockchain assisted by artificial intelligence, ensuring security and speed without the need for excessive power consumption. The UBIJ system would allow the entire world to receive a basic income without any government falling short of resources or going into debt.

What is UBIJ?

UBIJ is a guaranteed income for every person above the age of 5 in the world, along with job creation for adults and young adults who want to work. It is designed to address the challenges arising from automation and artificial intelligence, which are expected to eliminate many jobs. UBIJ is not limited to any particular country, ensuring that everyone receives it regardless of location.

Benefits of UBIJ

By providing a guaranteed income, UBIJ aims to eliminate poverty and reduce inequality. Additionally, it ensures that people can survive in a world where automation and artificial intelligence are rapidly changing the job market. The UBIJ system also levels the playing field for everyone, taking away the power of the elites and putting them on the same level as everyone else.

Implementation

Once a person reaches the age of 5, they will automatically start receiving UBIJ. The system would not be controlled by any government or individual, ensuring that everyone receives it equally, regardless of location. The UBIJ system would also encourage governments to prioritize the happiness of their residents, as they would have to ensure that their residents are satisfied to retain their wealth in their country.

How is UBIJ possible

With the current political and financial system, it is impossible. The only logical and intelligent way to do it is through a secure blockchain with a set of specific cryptocurrencies. Not just any blockchain or cryptocurrencies; the GlobeTrotter hybrid blockchain assisted by artificial intelligence, that can oversee the volume of transactions and security necessary to handle the whole World at the same time with a group of cryptocurrencies that include a stable coin and specialty tokens.

The new system would create and finance more local jobs like farmers, bakers, plumbers, mom & pop shops, etc. We would get back to basics where everybody can feel more fulfilled and useful again. Being a volunteer worker will be simpler now, helping people that need it thanks to **UBIJ**.

Which currency would be used and what is it backed by?

The main currency would be the GlobeTrotter Globie **GTC** coin ( )   Ǥ cryptocurrency along with a few other GlobeTrotter specialty tokens (details further down). The Globie could be backed by all the land in the world if it is decided that it needs to be backed by something.

What are the benefits of a Basic Income?

- **Eliminates the "unemployment trap".** Under current systems, when someone gets a job they lose most of their welfare payments. This means they can go from not working at all to working a full week without significantly increasing their income. This is a disincentive to work. Under basic income, when people get a job, they would retain the same basic income payment, with their salary added to it, so the disincentive no longer exists.

- **Reduces government bureaucracy.** A lot of government workers are required to ensure that welfare recipients are not claiming their benefits fraudulently, and to administer the complicated system of welfare payments and tax credits. The increased need for personal tax advisers also sucks skilled workers out of the productive sector. A basic income would hugely simplify the welfare system by replacing most of these bureaucracies, which would reduce its administrative costs significantly.

- **Ends personal taxes.** Taxes are too complicated and costly. Everything we can do to eliminate them would be, all things equal, a net gain in the value of human society. Predicting what tax bracket, you'll be in will no longer be necessary since personal income taxes will no longer exist for most people. Only the very rich will be paying personal taxes (a hoarding tax on their savings).

- **Drop sales tax.** There would only be sales tax on luxury items. There would not be any sales tax on any products or services that are included in basic needs for everyone. If people want and can afford luxury items, then they can afford the taxes.

- **Exemplifies and emphasizes single-class policymaking.** It is not structurally optimal to produce policies that explicitly divide people up into classes and then apply different laws to each class, as the bracketed tax code does (and as the welfare structure does). It is better to form a single law that applies to every individual on the planet: "Everyone gets $x in basic income, funded by a y% flat tax on companies". When we are all in the same 'group', class divisions become less divisive, and we reinforce the principles of liberty and equality.

- **Greatly reduces fraud/waste/abuse**. When welfare subsidies are contingent on conditions like employment, income level, number of hours worked, family status, etc., there are opportunities to game the system, either by illegally lying (fraud) or by simply obeying the economic incentives put in front of you (waste/abuse). These cause losses of real economic value, which are paid for by every taxpayer. Removing this incentive structure allows confidence in the welfare system's ability to reach people exactly as intended.

- **Guarantees a minimum living standard.** Though it's subjective/politicized, people may be entitled to a certain basic standard of living, regardless of whether they are momentarily able to participate in the labor market. Universal Declaration of Human Rights, Article 25, states, "Everyone has the right to a standard of living adequate for the health and well-being of himself and of his family, including food, clothing, housing and medical care and necessary social services, and the right to security in the event of unemployment, sickness, disability, widowhood, old age or other lack of livelihood in circumstances beyond his control." (United Nations, (UN)).

- **Increases bargaining power for workers.** Workers will be able to afford to refuse a job if the employer abuses its "cartel-like mindset" or the workspace has poor conditions, so firms will be forced to improve the employment conditions and wages for their workers. This will happen as a natural result of negotiation between firms and workers and will not require government intervention or unionization.

- **Lowers need for government regulations on the labor market.** Policies such as the minimum wage will become less necessary with the basic income, as people will already get enough money to live on from the basic income. And negotiating power for workers will increase. This will allow the government to remove some of the regulations on the labor market, creating a freer market and providing benefits for both employers and employees.

- **Deters undocumented immigration.** With the minimum wage obsolete, manual labor can be priced at its fair-market value, meaning undocumented immigrants will have to accept even lower wages to compensate for their legal risks, potentially putting the standard of life lower than if they stayed where they were.

- **Reduces the gender "pay gap".** Women, on average, make less money than men, and debaters of this issue fall into two camps: (1) those who want to reduce that gap to help women achieve financial freedom, and (2) those who want to prevent the harmful effects of government pay-mandates and micromanagement. Basic Income is capable of satisfying both camps by giving all citizens a base income, making women (and people in general) less dependent on their work-income. And it does so without removing any of the beneficial capitalistic incentives to work and provide value. Furthermore, the gender pay gap is reduced for precisely those women who most need it: low-income women. It makes them less dependent on a potentially abusive spouse and less sensitive to pregnancy-based work issues, without unjustly interfering with the market's ability to set salaries for upper and middle-class workers.

- **Improves mental health and security.** Mental health is one of the largest public health problems in most developed countries. The knowledge that the basic income will ensure a basic standard of living in any circumstances will provide a sense of mental security, especially when the economy is performing poorly. The removal of various dehumanising tests and stigmatisation of anyone who receives welfare payments will also serve to improve mental health. There is also evidence that poverty itself reduces cognitive capacity, comparable to a loss of 13 IQ points, or chronic alcoholism as compared to sobriety. A basic income would remove this cognitive impairment.

- **Increases physical health.** The rising cost of health care is a cause of great long-term concern, and basic income could lower this cost. In the Dauphin, Manitoba pilot experiment in Canada, an 8.5% reduction in hospitalization was found to be a direct result of the minimum income. This was attributed to the reduction in workplace injuries and family violence resulting from the rise in incomes.

- **Stabilizes costs over time.** Current welfare schemes have costs that fluctuate significantly with the performance of the economy and are increasing as the populations ages and more people leave the workforce. The costs of basic income schemes would not see this fluctuation, as the basic income is paid to all people* regardless of whether they are in the labor force or not.

- **Deals better with widespread unemployment.** Some people may argue that, with the development of new automation technology and the increase in the labour force due to globalisation, rates of unemployment in developed countries are likely to stay high and increase in coming years. This would impose a significant increased cost on current schemes, but as spending from the basic income would not increase, this system would be more able to cope with the change. Also, the long stressful wait to receive your first unemployment check would be eliminated.

- **Redistributes money from capital to labor.** Even if technology doesn't lead to high unemployment, it may well lead to lower wages and greater inequality. Capital, equipment and machinery that helps to produce things, is now creating a greater share of output compared to labour; human workers. This allows business owners, who own the capital, to pay workers the same or less while more is produced, so they make more profit for themselves. We are already seeing that output per worker is increasing, while workers' wages are not. In the long term, this will mean that business owners make more and more money, while those who don't own capital will make less and less. Basic income alleviates this by taxing the companies and the rich (who will probably own capital) and giving money to the poor (who probably won't), even if they can't find a job.

- **Increases number of small businesses.** Many people may currently be discouraged from leaving their job to start their own business, as if the venture fails, they will have no source of income. The basic income would provide income to these people, so more people would feel able to start businesses which could only increase innovation and competition in the economy. Evidence of this effect can be found in the Namibia basic income experiment, where those receiving it showed an increase in entrepreneurship with a 29% increase in average earned income, excluding the basic income. At the beginning of **UBIJ**, every adult will receive a big amount of "money" to help start a business if they wish. Every other person will also receive this, one-time, big amount once they reach adulthood.

- **Increases charitable work and academic research.** Much work in the charitable sector and other vocations (e.g., open-source programming, academia, or the arts) is socially beneficial but not profitable, so people have to do it in their spare time, along with a traditional job. A basic income would allow these people to spend more time on work that is socially beneficial but normally unprofitable for the individual.

- **Increases number of people in jobs they enjoy.** As people will not be forced to take on a job, they will be more able to find a job that they enjoy (or that pays well enough to offset their lack of enjoyment). Having people in jobs that suit them better will help improve mental health, as well as leading to an improved quality of goods and services.

- **Gives financial independence to all adults.** Every adult will be entitled to the basic income independently of any other people. This means they cannot be controlled or manipulated by someone through control of their finances, allowing people in abusive relationships to escape them more easily.

- **Helps families be happier and more independent.** The first two children of each family will also receive UBIJ to help pay for their needs without weighing on the family unit. Half of the UBIJ will be available for the parents to use for their children and the other half will be frozen until the children are 16 and old enough to manage their own finances.

- **Prevents generational theft.** Most western countries already provide basic income to people of retired age. But, if a nation or its socialized retirement program goes bankrupt or the socialized retirement program otherwise becomes unaffordable (most likely within 10 years due to fiscal mismanagement or simple birth rate demographics), then it is to the great advantage of current benefit recipients and at the total cost to those who pay into the benefits today with the false promise of receiving them in the future. If entitlements are unaffordable/unsustainable, then the only fair solution is to provide the funds equally today.

- **Leverages the multiplier effect.** "The mechanism that can give rise to a multiplier effect is that an initial incremental amount of spending can lead to increased consumption spending, increasing income further and hence further increasing consumption, etc., resulting in an overall increase in national income greater than the initial incremental amount of spending." It is this same effect that is seen in the differences to the economy the effects of $1 being spent by high income earners versus low-income earners have. As published in a recent report, "All those dollars low-wage workers spend create an economic ripple effect. Every extra dollar going into the pockets of low-wage workers, standard economic multiplier models tell us, adds about $1.21 to the national economy. Every extra dollar going into the pockets of a high-income American, by contrast, only adds about 39 cents to the GDP." This means a basic income could show this same multiplier effect on the entire economy by redistributing money from high earners to low and middle earners where the effects of spending are amplified.

Programs that could be cut with UBIJ

Some programs could be cut because of **UBIJ** but the moneys saved will be able to be put to better use. Governments will be getting the necessary amounts every month to supply all the benefits they need to offer their citizens, so these services are no longer needed:

- Welfare/workfare
- Business tax deductions/credits/subsidies
- Unemployment insurance
- Government pensions
- National minimum wage laws

How this will work

Who will receive UBIJ?

We will be giving every adult in the World Ǥ10,000 Globies in the beginning (or on their 18th birthday), then Ǥ1500 per month. There will be Ǥ300 per month to every young person between the ages of 5 and 17.

How this will be funded

- By charging a 30% tax to EVERY business in the World (25% going for **UBIJ** and 5% going to the local governments). Thus, eliminating any tax havens and companies moving out of a country because they can pay less elsewhere.
- By charging a 15% tax on luxury items going right to the local governments.
- By having a 10% hoarding tax on savings thus charging 10% on any savings (for individuals & companies) over a certain amount (like Ǥ1,000,000?) (Going to **UBIJ**).
- By having a 25% tax on any currency coming into a wallet (over a certain amount and a limited number of deposits that isn't from a regular income like from **UBIJ** or a regular salary under a certain amount) like big gifts, inheritances, winnings, etc. (20% for **UBIJ** and 5% for governments).
- By renting out all land worldwide and putting all the money back into the **UBIJ** system.

What security measures would be taken to make it tamper proof?

- The whole system will be automated on a hybrid blockchain, uncontrollable and unstoppable by any government or person.
- Everybody on the planet will be issued a unique ID kept private on the hybrid blockchain using a multimodal biometric identification.

- The system will run itself and not be influenced by anybody or any government without a proper vote.
- There will be a Justice Force that will take care of anybody abusing the system or stealing from others. Again, everything will be by vote on the blockchain. It will be instant justice, no more courts to slow the process down or let the rich & powerful get away with things they shouldn't. Nobody will be immune to the Justice Force.

What will happen with the banks?

- Every central, public and private bank on the planet can and will be shut down and used for something else.
- Every person's bank account will have the amount recorded just before the official announcement of **UBIJ** and people will receive the equal amount to what they were holding in the bank. There will be safeguards in place so that they cannot claim more coins than they should.

What about inflation?

Since every business will be accepting Globies, they will need to have a wallet and an API for their systems. Every API will have a serial number and will be controlled by the blockchain which in turn is controlled by the general population through voting. If companies abuse the system or exaggerate, people can vote and have that company's ability to accept tokens suspended, taxed or even shut down if it happens often enough. This system will give back the power to the people where it belongs.
Since there will be less people working, more machines, and other factors, inflation will be not non-existent. Machines do not require more money and people should be paid the same amount for doing the same job. Any increase in salary should come from profit sharing or a new higher position.

Inflation is a by-product of greed and wanting more for doing the same job and governments printing money like there is no tomorrow.

The consequences of having the Globie as the global currency

If everyone and every government on the planet agreed to use the Globie for trade, it would have significant implications for the global economy and financial systems. Here are some potential consequences:

1. **Universal acceptance:** With global agreement, the Globie would become a universally accepted medium of exchange. This could simplify international trade, reducing the need for currency conversions and associated fees.

2. **No transaction costs:** Cryptocurrencies generally offer lower transaction fees compared to traditional payment systems and the Globie would have no fees. Universal adoption would lead to significant cost savings for businesses and consumers for transactions including in cross-border transactions.

3. **Increased financial inclusion:** The Globie can provide access to financial services for people who are unbanked or underbanked, particularly in developing countries. A universally accepted cryptocurrency like the Globie would further promote financial inclusion.

4. **Enhanced security and privacy:** The Globie which is based on blockchain technology, offers increased security and privacy compared to traditional financial systems. Universal adoption could lead to more secure transactions and financial privacy for users.

5. **Greater transparency:** The Globie offers a high level of transparency since transactions are recorded on a public ledger. This could reduce corruption and improve trust in the global financial system.

6. **Monetary policy implications:** If the Globie were to replace all national currencies, governments would lose control over monetary policy. This could have positive implications. On one

hand, it could eliminate the risk of currency manipulation and inflation caused by government policies. Plus, it would limit governments' ability to overspend.

7. **Economic power shifts:** The widespread adoption of the Globie could shift economic power away from countries that currently have dominant currencies (such as the United States and the European Union). This could have geopolitical implications and affect international relations in a positive way.

8. **Decentralization:** By removing control from central banks and governments, the Globie would lead to a more decentralized financial system, making it more resistant to manipulation and corruption.

9. **No more inflation:** The Globie with a predetermined and transparent monetary policy would help eliminate the risk of inflation, as the money supply would be more predictable and not subject to government intervention.

10. **Empowerment of individuals:** A decentralized financial system could empower individuals by giving them more control over their finances and the ability to vote on important matters through blockchain technology.

11. **Efficient markets:** We could eliminate bailouts. Without government bailouts, failing businesses would not be artificially propped up, potentially leading to more efficient markets where resources are allocated based on merit and performance.

12. **Eliminate tax evasion:** A transparent and traceable Globie would make it impossible for individuals and businesses to evade taxes, resulting in increased government revenue.

13. **Universal Basic Income (UBI):** The Globie system would incorporate a mechanism for providing UBI, ensuring a basic level of financial security for all individuals worldwide.

14. **Better allocation of government resources:** With increased revenue from reduced tax evasion, governments might have more funds available to allocate towards social programs, infrastructure, and other public goods.

15. **Financial inclusion:** The Globie with UBI could further promote financial inclusion by providing access to basic financial resources for people in developing countries or those who were unbanked.

16. **Reduced income inequality:** The implementation of UBI and more equitable access to financial resources could help reduce income inequality and promote economic mobility.

17. **Stimulating economic growth:** By providing a stable, secure, and transparent financial system, the Globie would encourage investment and trade, fostering global economic growth.

18. **Enhanced government transparency:** A global cryptocurrency could improve transparency in government spending, making it easier for citizens to hold their governments accountable for the allocation of public funds.

19. **Environmental benefits:** If the hybrid blockchain technology used for the Globie addresses energy consumption concerns, the system could potentially have a lower environmental impact compared to traditional financial systems and some existing cryptocurrencies.

The GlobeTrotter Benefits

Wallet

Each individual wallet will be held on a mobile phone or tablet. Most people will have their wallet on their mobile phone and most companies will probably have their wallet on a tablet or computer. The balance is always in the wallet so no matter what, you always have all your money with you. The phone will update the blockchain every time it connects to the internet. The phone and the blockchain will do their checks and balances to make sure everything balances. The business wallets will be able to have multiple users, each using their own ID to make transactions for the company. This way, everybody knows what everybody else is doing in the company. The private transactions will not be available for companies.

A lost phone does not mean a lost wallet. If lost, getting a new phone, and setting it up with your biometrics means your wallet is automatically updated on your new phone with the same quantity of tokens you had in the old phone but all new tokens and coins whereas the old ones are burned on the blockchain. If just changing phones, you will be able to transfer all the tokens from the old phone to the new one.

Eliminating personal income tax

This system will allow the governments to receive more than enough coins from the taxes collected from the businesses and luxury taxes to cover all expenses thus eliminating personal income taxes for all. Plus, governments are able to keep their different programs running. The people are the ones that will be voting on how and where that tax money is spent.

The 5% taxes collected from the businesses and individuals getting big amounts (that are not **UBIJ** or salaries) and the 15% luxury tax, will go to the government where the people are registered as residing. This should eliminate illegal immigrants since everybody is getting money and it is in the country's best interest to let as many people register in their country as possible. Governments will be making their countries more attractive to foreigners and doing everything they can to keep the residents they have, happy.

Past Debt

Debt is not real since the banks created "money" out of thin air so every debt to any financial institution in the World will be erased. People will no longer owe money to banks or credit card companies for anything they own. Future debt will only be allowed up to a certain percentage of income. Every business in the World will be able to accept Lay-a-way plans. People need to live within their means which will only make people healthier and happier not having the weight of debt always on their minds.

GlobeTrotter Credit Cards

GlobeTrotter will give out credit cards to people 16 years old and older. They will come with a low maximum credit amount and will be able to go higher if the system deems the holder capable and responsible enough. The payments will be taken automatically every month by smart contract directly from their **UBIJ**. GlobeTrotter will teach everybody responsible spending and saving. There will be no interest charges on the credit nor any charges to the merchants accepting the Credit Cards.

Energy Companies

To promote a more equitable energy system, it is proposed that every energy company, including those that provide gas, oil, electric power, and other forms of energy, should become publicly owned and operated. This would ensure that prices are fair, while still allowing the company to make a reasonable profit that can be put back into the UBIJ system.

This proposal seeks to address the issue of companies that took advantage of people before, as they will no longer exist under this system. These companies will not be compensated for their businesses since they have already exploited the planet's resources and profited from something that did not belong to them in the first place. This approach aims to promote a more ethical and sustainable energy system that benefits everyone, rather than a select few.

Loans

Private loans between individuals will be possible with a maximum of 5% yearly interest.

If the loan was for building a business and the owner defaults on the loan, the business would belong to the lender, but the lender would have to pay a certain amount of what he received back to the borrower. The two parties will be able to negotiate a new contract if they wish to continue the arrangement.

If the loan is for a service business, artist or invention, the borrower will need to put up collateral for the loan or workout a deal of a % of every sale through a smart contract. If the borrower defaults, the lender would become half owner of whatever was being made.

Unique ID system

GlobeTrotter will give a smartphone to everyone that needs one. We will offer everybody on the planet a chance to get their own official ID, free of charge, to be able to receive their **UBIJ** payments and participate in any government programs available to them using their phone. The system will use a combination of face, retina, and fingerprint recognition and be updated every 5 years on their birthday.

Each person will need 1 person to vouch for them and be responsible for them. People cannot vouch for each other. One person cannot vouch for more than 20 people.

There will be information needed to make sure that everybody is known. There will be no secret identities and anybody wanting to collect **UBIJ**, or even use the GlobeTrotter system, will need to prove their identity.

At birth, the two parents (or the doctor and one parent) will create a new wallet for the child and at one year old, the child, with the help of his parent(s) will be required to input the necessary biometrics into his/her wallet.

<u>Death and leaving your estate to others</u>

When a person is living, they will be asked to choose a person as their executor. That executor will receive a special Executor token. When a person dies, a coroner will send a special token to the wallet of the dead person indicating that the owner is dead. The wallet will then reach out to the executor and ask for the Executor token. Now, the executor will have access to the deceased person's wallet.

<u>Voting System (accountability)</u>

The voting system will be available to everyone. It will be for voting on:

- Abusers*
- Companies that are charging too much or acting poorly
- Improvements on the system
- How and where taxes are spent by the governments
- People that aren't bringing anything positive to the community/World
- And many other things

*The people will also decide on the punishment through voting.

Voters will get paid for voting.

The benefits of this system

- Limiting the number of homes, a person or company can own.

- Being able to regulate big tech companies like Facebook, Twitter, Google, and others.
- Eliminating lobbying.
- Being able to fine, limit or close a company that abuses or endangers people or the environment.
- **Give a phone to everyone that needs one and expand wireless internet service Worldwide and having every blockchain transaction be free of charge (no internet fee).**
- Strengthen antitrust standards for companies.
- Limit markup prices.
- Eliminating discrimination and racism through education.
- No more need for passports.
- No more subsidies, government contracts, sub-contracting for governments (No more: private jails/prisons, schools for profit, private healthcare, etc.).
- Governments will run the businesses that supply essential services (Health care, schooling, cable tv, phone service, food markets, clothing manufacturers, etc.).
- No more supreme court as we know it.
- No more stock markets as we know them. They will be replaced with something else, but all the shares will be non-voting and the share holders have NO influence over the company. Companies cannot buy back their shares and the number of shares (of a certain company) per wallet will be limited.
- The percentage of extra taxes a company pays will be in ratio with the difference between the CEO/owner's pay and the typical worker's pay.
- The investment portfolios will be taxed every year on the value of it at that time.
- Regulate ALL markets; like no more than 10% profits for anything health related or anything essential.

<u>Problems that would be solved</u>

- No more cryptocurrency volatility.
- No more credit card frauds.
- No more ESG nonsense.
- No more climate change scare tactics.
- No more corrupt government officials.
- No more malfeasance, bribery, kickbacks influence-peddling.
- No more governments telling people what to do.
- No more problems for whistle blowers.
- No more election fraud.
- No more foreign governments causing problems in other countries.
- No more need for tariffs.
- No more corrupt justice officials.
- No more organized crime syndicates.
- No more terrorist groups like Antifa or BLM.
- No more tax evasion possible for companies.
- No more ruining the environment.
- No more raping the natural resources.
- No need for central banks or any banks for that matter.
- No more money laundering.
- No more terrorist financing.
- No more Jails.
- No more tax breaks for the rich and the big corporations.
- No more subsidies for companies/industries that don't really need them. If they can't compete within a free market, too bad.
- No more bank frauds.
- No more interest rate manipulations.
- No more mortgages and large debts.
- No more forex frauds or manipulations.
- No more governments spying on their citizens.
- No more sweatshops.

- No more CIA, FBI, NSA and all other "security" organizations and worldwide equivalents.
- **No more WARS**.
- No more spending on the military.
- No more armies.
- Free commuting on buses and trains
- Free schooling for life and all schools are non-profit
- Free childcare
- Free healthcare
- All salaries, incomes and expenditures will be public on the blockchain. This should cut down on inequality
- And the list goes on…

Open markets

There can be a return of real open markets. People will have the possibility of voting for what they want available or banned in their city, state, country, World. People caught selling or bringing in unwanted products/services in a protected area will be penalized. There will be designated areas for drugs, prostitution, and gambling. People will be allowed to go there BUT every expenditure made there will be visible on the blockchain.

Innovation

Innovation will be encouraged by granting free international patents to everyone that has an idea/invention that qualifies. 20% of their royalties will be going back into the **UBIJ**. Every patent will be on a smart contract and people will be automatically paid for the use of their ideas.

Abusers

Abusers will be voted against by their peers. The punishments can be anywhere from a fine to being banned from a country, or worse if they are proven to not bring anything positive to the society. It will start with the person paying back double what they took, back to the people involved. Then, after another abuse, maybe shipped to a country/island with other abusers (to be determined and voted on).

Governments abusing in any way will be voted on and can be removed from power. If individuals in government are voted guilty, they will be treated like any other abuser. There will be no one above the rules or the punishments.

Future Jobs

We don't know what the future holds but one thing is for sure, there will be less jobs because of AI and automation. There will always be a need for people in certain jobs and because of **UBIJ**, the job perks will need to be good and the bosses as well since the people will have the luxury of being able to refuse a job.

The initial payment from **UBIJ** should be enough to help start many small local businesses and create jobs.

Relief Funds

Relief funds will be always available to help areas that have been hit by natural disasters or because of human destruction. These funds will be voted on by everyone.

Land

THE PLANET BELONGS TO EVERYBODY. No person or government really owns any land. This way, there will be no more land ownership for anybody. Anybody living on a piece of land will pay rent to the rest of the World for that piece of land for his or her dwelling/business/usage of it. People lease the land from the planet (**UBIJ**) and can only sell what they have built or improved on the land. All leases would be put up for vote through a smart contract and if people do not respect their smart contract, they lose the use of the land and their deposit. Existing ownership will be recognized as a 100-year lease. The piece of land can never be sold, only the property that is built on it.

Land rental price will depend on what it will be used for, size and natural resources. People that used to work in certain positions in the government but are no longer needed because of **UBIJ**, will be able to continue working and evaluating land for the rental price.

Housing

Homes will be built for everyone by the **UBIJ** system, thus creating jobs, and these homes will be on a rent-to-own basis and the rental income will be used for building new homes. There will be a maximum number of homes a person or company can own thus ending any control issues.

Rental prices for other buildings not owned by the **UBIJ** system will be governed and regulated as to control landlords that typically abuse their power. Any landlord caught neglecting and/or abusing will face consequences.

Natural resources

Land will be leased to excavation companies through voting. Anybody excavating land for the natural resources needs to respect the environment otherwise they lose the right to excavate and the right to rent any other piece of land. The piece of land that is being used needs to be better than when the excavating company first got there.

Governments

All governments will go back to the way they were meant; to serve the public and take care of things that we do not want to do or have time to do.

Since everything will be simplified, governments can be downsized and become more efficient.

The differences between today's blockchain systems and the GlobeTrotter system

Cryptocurrencies and blockchains are the future and are greatly needed and have many upsides to them but they have their down sides too. Here, we will address how GlobeTrotter Cryptocurrency will resolve these problems.

Adoption by the masses

Right now, people are mostly using cryptocurrencies for speculation and investment purposes. Cryptocurrencies are too volatile for merchants to accept and possibly too profitable as an investment for consumers to use.

The solution is a stable cryptocurrency, and the GlobeTrotter Globie coin is the only truly stable coin. It will be attractive to both merchants and consumers because of it always having the exact same value. This is the key to a cryptocurrency being adopted and used by the masses.

Difficult to understand

There is a big learning curve to understanding and using cryptocurrency. Things need to be more user friendly and intuitive.

GlobeTrotter will have a simple to use interface that will feel familiar to people. Straightforward, simple, and logical.

The loss of wallets

People losing their wallets (for reasons like hacks, computer crash, losing their computer or phone, etc.) are a reality and a big downside right now.

GlobeTrotter will have a backup system in place to recover lost wallets and private keys. This is something that is easily implemented and greatly needed in the cryptocurrency world.

The loss of funds

People and businesses being hacked happens. Right now, anybody that loses their coins from being hacked doesn't have the chance of getting them back. Once they are gone, they are gone for good.

GlobeTrotter will have a system that will let them block the stolen coins from being used and replace them back to the original owners. Through our PIN system, the stolen coins are rendered useless without the PIN number and it also gives us time to blacklist the stolen coins in case they can crack the PIN number.

Government/Police Seizure Protection

Illegal government and police seizures are a very real possibility. Many countries like the USA have "legalized" illegal seizures of property. With the new laws saying that you have to declare carrying over $10,000 worth of cryptocurrency when entering the country, they can seize it if you don't declare it and even if you declare it. Technically, nobody can carry cryptocurrency, it's on the blockchain, but that won't stop them.

Our wallets will have a pin number that is required to open it. They will also have an emergency pin number that, if entered, will show your balance as whatever you want it to.

Purchase protection

When purchasing something online with cryptocurrency, you need to completely trust the merchant because once you send him your coins, they are his and if he doesn't send you the product, you lose.

GlobeTrotter has developed their "Smarter Contract System" that will let consumers easily create a contract that if not respected by the merchant, they are refunded. This new system eliminates possibilities of fraud.

Scalability

Most blockchains have scaling issues which result in slower confirmation times as it gets busier. The more people on a blockchain, the slower it gets and the more expensive it gets.

GlobeTrotter's hybrid blockchain (T-Chain) will be the opposite. The more people use it, the faster and more secure it gets. Through our combination of different technologies, we plan to solve every problem present blockchains are having. This "T-Chain" is the ultimate decentralized solution.

No real advantages in purchasing with cryptocurrencies today

Right now, there aren't really any advantages to purchasing anything with cryptocurrency. It won't cost you anything less and most merchants that do accept cryptos go through a third party like Coinbase to transfer the purchase to FIAT currency and pay fees.

GlobeTrotter will not charge any fees when paying with or transferring Globies.

Developers and miners

Every cryptocurrency and blockchain is dependent on the developers and miners and when those two disagree, there is a fork. That affects the value of the coins/tokens and we can only sit back and watch.

The GlobeTrotter Ecosystem will be the way it should have been from the start. There will be no possibility of a fork. Anything added to the system will be voted on by all token holders and anything that is put up for vote can only have upsides. It is especially important to GlobeTrotter that everybody always comes out ahead.

Debit cards

Right now, there are dozens of cryptocurrency debit cards but they aren't really solving any problems. They actually cost the consumer more than using a bank debit card and the merchants still have to pay the same fees. One important reason for cryptocurrency's reason for being is to cut out the middleman. These debit cards are just middlemen on a blockchain. Plus, who really wants to spend a coin that is going up in value? Almost nobody.

GlobeTrotter eliminates the need for debit cards. Everything will be on your phone.

Privacy

Most blockchains show every transaction on them and even though it is wallet number to wallet number and there are no names attached to any of them, most remain traceable by people who know what they are doing. Not everybody wants that info out there so GlobeTrotter has added a privacy option on every transaction through its "Smarter Contract System." It lets only the two people involved in the transaction to be able to view it on the T-Chain. There will be a limit on how many private transactions you can have. Only a member of the Justice Force will have access to the private transaction but only with serious doubts of elicit behaviour.

Big ICO's slowing down the blockchains and making coins even more volatile

The problem with big ICO's is that they slow down the blockchains of the participating cryptocurrencies. Also, when all those buyers are acquiring coins to buy into the ICO's, the price goes up and when comes time for those ICO's to cash out, they make the market drop again creating a very volatile scenario.

With the Globie coin, ICO's will be able to collect funds that will always have the same value. No worries of it dropping in value overnight. If the ICO's use Globie coins instead of BTC, ETH or any other, they won't be overloading those blockchains and it will also help in stabilizing those coins plus, there are no fees.

Smart Contracts

Smart contracts are fantastic, and their usefulness is endless but to make smart contracts right now, you need to be a programmer in that language. To use smart contracts, you need to write one or refer to an existing one on the blockchain. There are millions of possibilities to have in smart contracts so keeping track of all of them is nearly impossible.

GlobeTrotters' solution is simpler. Every token has a smart contract embedded into it. Using the GlobeTrotter Wallet with the "Smarter Contract System" built into it, you can create a smart contract as easily as checking off whichever conditions you want on the list, adding dates and times and more. This lets you include any condition you want for the transaction to be complete. The receiver will see a copy of the contract and have the choice to accept it, refuse it or suggest changes.

THE TECHNOLOGY

The blockchain

The blockchain will be a hybrid blockchain by using the best of a decentralized and private blockchain technology to create a super secure and super fast 100% decentralized blockchain. This blockchain cannot be manipulated by outside forces other than everything being voted on by the citizens of the World. There will be fail-safes in place as to not be able to vote for a higher UBI wage for everyone UNLESS the system can afford it over time, and other contingencies. The blockchain will be assisted by artificial intelligence. The blockchain will be free to use, meaning no cost to make any transactions or transfers.

The crypto tokens and coins

- **GTC coin:** This coin (Globie) will be the currency used for all purchases. It will have a constant value because there will no longer be any inflation. There will be a limited amount of GTC coins in the system albeit a huge number of them.

- **GTP token:** This NFT token will be used for property ownership and transfers. Anybody will be able to mint a GTP with their property token and transfer their property to the blockchain if wanted where it can be kept, sold, or traded.

- **GTV token:** This NFT token will be used for voting. Everybody will receive a bunch of tokens for voting. These tokens will represent each individual. This way, the blockchain knows who owns the token and each person can only vote once per vote. This token is not transferable to others. Once a voting token is used, it is burned.

- **GTA token:** This NFT token will be used for admissions to replace tickets. Venues with shows or admittance requirements will mint GTA tokens to sell them or give them away.

- **GGT token:** This NFT token will be used as a gift token or a coupon token. Its purpose will be for promotional use for gifts, rewards, bonuses, etc. Each business will be able to mint them for their own business and send them out to whoever or give them out on their website.

- **GTE token:** This NFT token will be used to choose an executor. This token can only be sent back to the original owner. If the holder dies, the GTE token will be automatically sent back to the original owner.

- **GTI token:** This NFT token will be used as an ID token whenever you need to send someone your details or prove who you are. This token would be used when creating a new wallet for a newborn among other things, open an account, or retrieve an account.

The Smarter Contract System

Every coin/token will have a "Smarter Contract" imbedded into it to let the users define the conditions when sending and/or receiving them. The "Smarter Contracts" are part of the coin and not a separate entity on the blockchain like most other smart contracts. Why "Smarter Contract"? Because it is extremely simple to use and a smarter way to use smart contracts. To define what the conditions that need to be fulfilled are for the coins, the user will just need to check off the desired choices from a list. It will be an extremely user-friendly system.

Security

Unlike all cryptocurrencies today, if the wallet or private keys are lost, they will be recoverable. If the wallet is hacked and coins/tokens are stolen without the smarter contract being filled out (which only the owner can do), they will be recovered and placed back into your wallet.

There will be many safeguards in the system making it impossible to steal coins. Also, the smarter contracts will eliminate chargebacks protecting the merchants from fraud.

The Reform of most industries

Stock markets will be eliminated all together and replaced with a more equitable system that cannot be manipulated. The stock markets were created by the rich **FOR** the rich just to further their wealth by cheating the system. The stock markets no longer have anything to do with reality. The stock markets will be replaced by a new system that will use strict rules that everyone will have to follow being that it will run on the blockchain and there will be no way to cheat or fix the system.

- **Immutable and Transparent Transactions:**
The new stock market systems will leverage the power of blockchain technology to ensure all transactions are recorded in an immutable and transparent manner. Every trade will be permanently stored on the blockchain, providing a comprehensive and auditable transaction history.

- **Smart Contracts for Compliance:**
Compliance with regulatory requirements will be enforced through smart contracts deployed on the blockchain. These self-executing contracts will automatically validate and enforce compliance rules, ensuring fair and consistent treatment of market participants.

- **Decentralized Governance and Voting:**
A decentralized governance model will be implemented, allowing market participants to actively participate in decision-making processes. Through secure voting mechanisms on the blockchain, stakeholders will collectively determine rules, punishments, and regulatory changes.

- **Whistleblower Protection:**
The new system will prioritize the protection of whistleblowers by employing advanced cryptographic techniques and pseudonymity.

Whistleblowers will be able to report misconduct anonymously, ensuring their safety while providing critical information for investigations.

- **Immutable Complaint System:**

A transparent and immutable complaint system will be integrated into the blockchain platform. This system will securely record and track complaints, ensuring transparency, accountability, and fairness in addressing grievances and disputes.

- **Global Economic System:**

A unified global economic system will be established on the blockchain, featuring a single currency for seamless cross-border transactions. This system will foster economic integration and stability, eliminating complexities associated with multiple currencies.

- **Efficient Dispute Resolution:**

Dispute resolution processes will be streamlined through the use of smart contracts and decentralized arbitration mechanisms. The blockchain's immutable records and tamper-resistant nature will ensure fair and efficient resolution of conflicts.

- **AI-Powered Market Surveillance:**

Advanced AI algorithms will be employed for real-time market surveillance, detecting patterns of market manipulation, insider trading, and fraudulent activities. AI will act as a vigilant overseer, ensuring market integrity and investor protection.

- **AI-Driven Risk Assessment:**

AI models will assess and quantify risks associated with different investments, portfolios, and market conditions. Investors will benefit from personalized risk analysis, empowering them to make well-informed investment decisions.

- **AI-Enabled Investor Education:**

AI-powered educational tools and platforms will provide personalized investment guidance, empowering investors with knowledge and insights tailored to their individual profiles. This AI-driven education will foster financial literacy and responsible investment practices.

- **AI-Enhanced Market Efficiency:**

AI algorithms will optimize trade execution, improving liquidity and reducing transaction costs. By analyzing market data and participant behavior, AI will enhance market efficiency and promote fair and timely trade execution.

- **AI-Powered Investor Protection:**

AI models will proactively identify and flag potential investor vulnerabilities, providing early warning systems for scams or fraudulent schemes. This AI-powered investor protection will safeguard individuals from financial exploitation.

EDUCATIONAL SYSTEM

- **An Emphasis on Factual Learning & Intellectual Freedom:**

Discarding divisive and counterproductive ideologies such as DEI programs, loyalty tests, and Critical Race Theory, the revised educational framework will instead promote intellectual freedom and factual learning. Education should not be about indoctrinating students with a certain worldview, but about expanding their minds and encouraging independent thinking. It is through this emphasis on critical thinking, not what to think, but how to think, that we can mold our future generations into discerning, compassionate, and engaged citizens.

- **Critical Thinking & Logical Reasoning:**

Right from their formative years, students will be immersed in an educational environment that prioritizes the development of critical thinking skills and logical reasoning. Instruction in the principles of logic, the art of reasoning, and the rigours of the scientific method will be integral to their learning journey. They will be equipped to question, to debate, and to evaluate the credibility of sources. This foundational skillset will permeate every subject they tackle, enabling them to critically analyze and scrutinize all information they encounter throughout their lives.

-   **Balanced and Inclusive History Curriculum:**
The study of history will take center stage in our proposed curriculum, providing students with a broad understanding of diverse political systems, the intrinsic value of individual freedoms, and the perilous nature of totalitarian regimes. History will not be taught through a narrow, divisive lens, but rather with a focus on shared human experiences and the lessons we can learn from them. The aim is to instil in students an appreciation for democratic, just and fair values and to underscore the pivotal role of vigilant, informed citizenship in safeguarding these liberties.

-   **Entrepreneurship & Economic Acumen:**
To cultivate self-reliance and foster a spirit of independence, students will be introduced to the fundamentals of entrepreneurship and economic literacy. They'll gain insights into the intricacies of budgeting, the art of investing, the inescapable reality of taxes, and the foundational elements of initiating and managing a business. These essential, real-world skills will empower them to adeptly steer their financial futures and confidently navigate the economic dimensions of their lives.

-   **Practical Self-sufficiency Skills:**
In addition to academic subjects, the curriculum will incorporate practical skills essential for self-sufficiency. This could span from the therapeutic art of gardening, rudimentary home repair techniques, the culinary science of cooking, basic first aid proficiency, to a host of other survival skills. This comprehensive approach aims to equip students with the necessary competencies to be self-sustaining in various facets of life.

- **Promotion of Open Discourse & Debate:**
Classroom environments will be nurtured to foster open discourse and lively debates, providing students with a platform to freely articulate their thoughts and viewpoints. This will cultivate an atmosphere of intellectual curiosity, nudging students to delve into diverse perspectives and formulate their own well-informed opinions.

- **Customized Learning Trajectories:**
Acknowledging the distinctiveness of each student, the educational system will advocate for tailored learning trajectories. This method will enable students to explore their individual interests and talents, thereby kindling a passion for learning and facilitating personal growth.

- **Teacher Training & Support:**
Educators will be provided with comprehensive training to equip them with these novel teaching methodologies and subject matter. They will also receive continuous support and resources to hone their skills and adapt to the evolving educational landscape. However, educators advocating for transgender ideologies and similar narratives will no longer be permitted in the educational system.

- **Whole-Person Development:**
The educational system should cherish and cultivate all facets of a child's development, including their physical health, mental and emotional well-being, social aptitude, artistic creativity, and beyond. This could involve integrating physical education, the arts, mindfulness practices, and more into the day-to-day curriculum.

- **Global Economics & Monetary Acumen:**
In the transformed global economic system with a single currency and no traditional banks, students will be educated on the system's unique dynamics and personal financial management. They'll comprehend how this unified currency impacts worldwide trade, economics, and personal wealth, as well as the influence of economic policies. They'll learn to

balance expenses, savings, and investments and understand the significance of secure digital transactions, individual accountability, and transparency in this new system. The goal is to equip them with the skills to make informed decisions that promote their financial stability and positively impact the global community.

FOOD & BEVERAGE INDUSTRY

- **Transparency in Labeling:**
Consumers should know exactly what they're eating. Implement stricter regulations on food and beverage labeling to ensure that all ingredients are listed clearly and accurately. This includes potentially harmful additives, preservatives, and artificial flavors or colors. A traffic light system could be introduced on packaging to indicate the healthiness of the product.

- **Encourage Local and Seasonal Produce:**
Promote the use of local, seasonal produce in food production. This not only reduces the environmental footprint of food transport but also tends to result in fresher and more nutritious products. Government incentives could be provided to businesses that source locally.

- **Eliminate Harmful Substances:**
Phase out the use of harmful substances such as trans fats, high-fructose corn syrup, and certain artificial sweeteners in food and beverage production. Establish strict limits on the amount of added sugars and sodium allowed in products.

- **Promote Organic Farming:**
Provide incentives for farmers to switch to organic farming methods, which are more sustainable and result in produce free from synthetic pesticides and fertilizers.

- **Regulate Marketing:**

Restrict misleading marketing tactics, particularly those targeting children. This could involve limiting the use of cartoon characters to market unhealthy foods and regulating the advertisement of certain products during children's TV programming.

- **Education and Public Awareness:**

Implement public awareness campaigns to educate consumers about the importance of a balanced diet, how to read food labels, and the potential health risks associated with certain ingredients.

- **Support Healthy Alternatives:**

Encourage the development and sale of healthier alternatives to popular food and beverage items. This could involve providing research and development grants or tax breaks to companies working on such products.

- **Mandatory Nutritional Education:**

Require restaurants and other food service establishments to provide nutritional information for all menu items to help consumers make informed choices.

PHARMACEUTICAL INDUSTRY

Reforming the pharmaceutical industry to emphasize transparency, value, and holistic healthcare solutions can be achieved using a diverse set of strategies. Here are some notable ones:

- **R&D Transparency**: Mandate that all clinical trials be registered, with results being publicized regardless of the outcome. An international database can be established for all clinical trial data, fostering consistency, and preventing redundancy. This ensures that patients and healthcare providers have comprehensive data on drug efficacy and safety.

- **Natural Remedies Research**: Ramp up funding towards investigating traditional and natural remedies. By establishing dedicated institutions that focus on this area and fostering partnerships between conventional and traditional medicine, we can provide a broader spectrum of healthcare solutions.

- **Pharmacovigilance Enhancement**: Build robust post-market surveillance systems that swiftly detect and address adverse drug reactions. The use of a global reporting system ensures that countries can promptly share data on newly discovered drug side effects, ensuring rapid global response.

- **Value-based Pricing**: Introduce drug pricing models that reflect the actual value provided to patients. By liaising with healthcare economists and patient advocacy groups, a more equitable pricing system can be established that ensures accessibility and affordability.

- **Promotion of Holistic Approaches**: Encourage medical institutions to adopt a preventive and root-cause approach to care. By integrating holistic health modules into curricula and pushing for public awareness, we can create a healthcare system that places as much emphasis on prevention as on cure.

- **Stricter Advertising Regulation**: Mandate rigorous vetting for pharmaceutical advertisements to ensure accuracy. By prohibiting direct-to-consumer advertising that doesn't provide a balanced perspective, consumers are better equipped to make informed decisions.

- **Public Education Initiatives**: Launch widespread public awareness campaigns about both synthetic and natural remedies. Community health programs and digital platforms can be harnessed to inform the public about drug usage, side effects, and natural alternatives.

- **Open-Source Drug Development**: Promote the establishment of open-source platforms for drug research, democratizing the process and reducing costs. International collaboration can ensure shared knowledge and resources are used optimally in drug development.

By adopting these strategies, the pharmaceutical industry can evolve into a more patient-centric, transparent, and holistic sector, emphasizing long-term health and well-being over short-term symptom relief.

MANUFACTURING INDUSTRY

- **Product Standards and Certifications:**
Develop rigorous standards for durability and longevity. Products that meet these standards could be awarded a certification, providing consumers with assurance of their quality and durability.

- **Shift to Circular Economy:**
Embrace the principles of the circular economy, which involves designing products to be used, reused, and recycled in a closed loop. This reduces waste and encourages manufacturers to build products that last longer.

- **Legislation Against Planned Obsolescence:**
Introduce laws to prevent planned obsolescence, the practice of designing products to become obsolete or stop working after a certain period to prompt consumers to buy the latest model.

- **Incentivize Long-Lasting Products:**
Implement a tax on products that are designed with a short lifespan and are difficult to repair.

- **Support for Research and Development:**
Invest in research and development to discover new materials and manufacturing processes that increase product longevity.

- **Right to Repair Laws:**

Implement right-to-repair laws that compel manufacturers to make their products repairable and to supply parts and documentation to independent repair shops.

- **Consumer Education:**

Launch initiatives to educate consumers about the cost benefits and environmental impact of purchasing long-lasting, repairable products versus disposable ones.

- **Sustainable Supply Chains:**

Encourage manufacturers to source materials responsibly and verify that their supply chains are sustainable. This not only ensures the ethical production of goods but can also contribute to product quality.

SERVICE INDUSTRY

- **Regulations and Standards:**

Implement comprehensive regulations and standards to govern the industry and establish benchmarks for efficiency, transparency, and customer satisfaction.

- **Customer Feedback Mechanisms:**

Encourage businesses to actively seek and respond to customer feedback. This can be facilitated through online reviews, satisfaction surveys, and complaint resolution mechanisms. All these will be on the blockchain and monitored.

- **Transparency in Pricing and Services:**

Mandate clear communication of pricing, terms of service, and any additional charges to prevent hidden fees or costs.

- **Professional Training and Development:**

Invest in comprehensive professional development programs to train employees in delivering exceptional customer service and efficient work practices.

- **Quality Certifications:**

Implement a system of quality certifications for businesses that consistently demonstrate high standards in efficiency, transparency, and customer satisfaction.

- **Strict Penalties for Violations:**

Enforce strict penalties for businesses that violate regulations or fail to meet the established standards, including fines, sanctions, or the revocation of business licenses in extreme cases.

- **Investment in Technology:**

Encourage businesses to leverage modern technologies to improve their service delivery, such as AI for customer service, blockchain for transparency, and data analytics for improving efficiency.

- **Independent Monitoring Bodies:**

Establish independent monitoring bodies to ensure compliance with the standards and to handle disputes and complaints from consumers.

HEALTHCARE INDUSTRY

- **Universal Access and Blockchain:**

Using blockchain technology, a decentralized and secure digital ledger, can help create a more transparent and efficient system for managing healthcare records, insurance claims, and payments, ensuring that everyone has access to essential healthcare services regardless of income or social status.

- **Preventive Care:**

The emphasis would still be on preventive care and wellness. Blockchain can play a role here by securely storing and sharing individual health data, enabling personalized preventive measures and early detection of potential health issues.

- **Quality Improvement:**

Standards of care across all healthcare providers could be monitored and maintained via the blockchain, ensuring that all data regarding treatment protocols, patient outcomes, and facility inspections are reliably recorded and accessible.

- **Efficiency and Innovation:**

Blockchain technology could streamline healthcare delivery by offering secure, immediate access to medical records, reducing administrative time and costs. Furthermore, innovations such as telemedicine and AI could be more effectively implemented with the secure data management offered by blockchain.

- **Transparency:**

Blockchain technology could increase transparency in pricing and outcomes, as all transactions would be recorded and viewable on the blockchain. This could enable patients to make more informed decisions and stimulate competition based on quality and cost-effectiveness.

- **Mental Health:**

Mental health services could be improved with the secure and private handling of sensitive mental health records on the blockchain, ensuring patient privacy while facilitating better coordination of care.

- **Holistic Approach:**

Treating the whole person could be facilitated by blockchain technology, as it allows for secure and efficient sharing of information between different care providers, including medical professionals, social services, nutritionists, and therapists.

- **Pharmaceutical Industry Reform and Blockchain:**

Blockchain can play a significant role in addressing the high cost of prescription drugs by tracing the supply chain, verifying the authenticity of drugs, and creating a more competitive and transparent marketplace.

Implementing these blockchain-enabled reforms could make the healthcare system more equitable, effective, and patient-centered.

TRANSPORTATION INDUSTRY

Reforming the transportation industry, while avoiding a heavy reliance on electric vehicles due to limited battery materials, could involve a range of strategies. Let's consider a few:

- **Decentralized Transit Systems:**

Implementing a blockchain-based system can facilitate the integration of various modes of public transport into a single, user-friendly network. This could include trains, buses, trams, shared electric bikes, and more. Commuters can use a single digital token to travel across the network, with fares automatically calculated and deducted based on the distance traveled.

- **On-Demand Shuttle Services:**

In suburban areas, where traditional public transport routes may not be practical, on-demand electric shuttle services could be deployed. These shuttles, which could be powered by renewable energy sources, could transport residents from their homes to central locations like train stations, shopping centers, or workplaces.

- **High-Speed Rail Systems:**
High-speed rail systems could be expanded to provide a faster and more eco-friendly alternative to long-distance car travel or short-haul flights. Blockchain could be used to streamline ticketing and payment, ensuring a seamless travel experience for passengers.

- **Non-Battery Electric Solutions:**
Explore non-battery electric solutions such as overhead or ground-level power lines for buses and trams, similar to what is currently used for some light rail systems. This eliminates the need for recharging and allows vehicles to run continuously.

- **Shared Mobility:**
Promote shared mobility services, which can drastically reduce the number of vehicles on the road. Blockchain technology could provide a secure, transparent platform for managing shared resources, whether it's a ride-hailing service or a community-owned fleet of vehicles.

- **Urban Planning:**
Encourage urban planning strategies that minimize the need for long commutes, such as mixed-use developments that integrate residential, commercial, and recreational spaces. This will reduce the overall demand for transportation.

- **Blockchain for Logistics:**
In freight transport, blockchain can provide end-to-end visibility and traceability, enhancing efficiency, and reducing fraud and errors. It can also facilitate smart contracts for automatic, transparent billing and payments.

- **Incentivization Programs:**
Use blockchain to implement and manage incentivization programs that encourage the use of public transport or shared mobility services. This

could be in the form of tokens that can be used to pay for rides, goods, or services within the network.

By leveraging these strategies, the transportation industry can be reformed in a way that enhances accessibility, efficiency, and sustainability, without over-relying on battery-powered vehicles

MENTAL HEALTH AND WELL-BEING INDUSTRY

- **Global Awareness and Education Campaigns:**
Launch worldwide campaigns to reduce the stigma around mental health. Use media, celebrities, and influencers to push for narratives that normalize seeking help and understanding mental health nuances.

- **Universal Training:**
Equip every individual, from school-going children to elderly populations, with basic mental health first aid training. This training would encompass understanding the signs of mental distress and the appropriate steps to assist or seek professional help.

- **Accessible Care:**
Utilize the blockchain and AI system to create a platform where people can connect with certified therapists and counselors from around the world, ensuring no barriers like language or geographical distance.

- **Tailored Therapy:**
Using AI, design therapy modules tailored to individual needs. This could also include AI-driven therapy bots for interim assistance until a human professional is available.

- **Holistic Approaches:**
Encourage methods that encompass mind, body, and spirit. This could mean integrating techniques like meditation, physical activity, and dietary recommendations alongside traditional therapy.

-   **Community Support Systems:**
Using the global platform, create support groups for various mental health challenges. Allow individuals to join, share, and find community in their struggles.

-   **Quality Control:**
With AI's help, continuously assess the quality and effectiveness of therapists and counselors. Ensure that only the most efficient, empathetic, and updated professionals are part of the system.

-   **Continuous Research:**
Fund global research initiatives to keep updating our understanding of mental health. Use AI to spot patterns, predict mental health crises, and develop preventive measures.

-   **Crisis Management:**
Design a fast-response system for individuals in acute distress. This could use both AI for immediate intervention and a human response team for critical situations.

-   **Holistic Growth Programs:**
Beyond immediate mental health needs, create programs that focus on holistic well-being, helping individuals find purpose, community, and joy.

CULTURAL PRESERVATION

In a world so unified and globalized, there could be challenges related to preserving individual cultures, languages, and traditions.

-   **Cultural Archives:**
Develop vast digital archives, leveraging the hybrid blockchain system, to store and document cultural practices, languages, art, folklore, and traditions. Allow communities to contribute and authenticate information, ensuring its accuracy and inclusivity.

- **Cultural Festivals and Exchanges:**

Establish global cultural festivals celebrated in various parts of the world. Encourage intercultural exchanges where individuals can learn about different cultures firsthand by visiting and interacting.

- **Localized Education:**

While a unified educational system has its merits, there should be segments of education dedicated to local history, culture, and traditions. Schools should emphasize the importance of cultural roots.

- **Support for Indigenous and Minorities:**

Prioritize the protection and promotion of indigenous communities and their ways of life. Recognize them as custodians of age-old traditions and knowledge.

- **Global Cultural Fund:**

Create a fund that financially supports initiatives aimed at cultural preservation, whether it's restoring old monuments, documenting dying languages, or supporting traditional artisans.

- **Digital Platforms for Artisans:**

Use the global platform to allow local artisans to showcase their traditional crafts and arts, connecting them to a worldwide audience and ensuring the survival of ancient craftsmanship.

- **Language Revival Initiatives:**

Recognize and document endangered languages. Launch initiatives, courses, and apps that teach these languages, encouraging global citizens to learn them, keeping them alive.

- **Media and Content:**

Encourage the production of content in local languages, telling local stories. Movies, series, books, and music in native languages would ensure that culture thrives in the modern age.

- **Cultural Research Grants:**

Offer grants for researchers studying different cultures, ensuring a deep understanding and appreciation of each culture's nuances.

- **Global Cultural Dialogues:**

Organize platforms where global dialogues on culture preservation are held, involving stakeholders from various parts of the world, ensuring every voice is heard.

DIGITAL PRIVACY AND AUTONOMY

Even with blockchain, there are issues of digital privacy, control over one's digital identity, and protection against potential misuse of AI.

- **Decentralized Digital Identities:**

Implement decentralized identity systems. Every individual controls their identity, with personal information stored on their devices, and only cryptographic proofs are shared, minimizing exposure.

- **Regular Audits of AI:**

Ensure that AI systems undergo frequent, perhaps quarterly, external audits. Transparency in their workings, decisions, and data-handling processes will be vital.

- **AI Ethics Framework:**

Establish a global ethics framework for AI, ensuring that every AI system adheres to these principles, preventing any misuse.

- **Opt-in Data Sharing:**

Data should only be shared with explicit consent, with users having the option to retract their data whenever they choose.

- **Educate on Digital Rights:**

Launch global campaigns that educate citizens on their digital rights. When people are informed, they can better protect their privacy.

- **Zero-Knowledge Proofs:**

Implement cryptographic methods like zero-knowledge proofs which allow one party to prove to another that a statement is true, without revealing any specific information about the statement itself.

- **Immutable Logs:**

Any access or change to personal data should be logged immutably on the blockchain. If there's any unauthorized access, it's visible and traceable.

- **Open-Source AI Models:**

Encourage the development and use of open-source AI models. When the code is publicly available, it's easier to spot biases, errors, or potential misuse.

- **Digital Ombudsman:**

Establish a digital ombudsman role at the global level, responsible for addressing grievances related to digital privacy and AI misuse.

- **Personal AI Guardians:**

Introduce personal AI systems for every individual, designed to protect the user's digital footprint, alert them of potential breaches, and ensure their digital autonomy.

- **Privacy by Design:**

Rather than bolting on privacy features, every digital tool and service should be built from the ground up with privacy as a core principle.

ETHICS OF AI

Potential challenges of superintelligent AI, their rights (if any), and preventing AI biases.

- **Framework of AI Principles:**

Establish a globally recognized framework of principles that every AI should be developed and operated under. This ensures that the primary design of AI is rooted in fairness, accountability, and transparency.

- **AI Rights Charter:**

Given the rise of superintelligent AI, create a charter that identifies the rights of such entities, especially if they attain a level of consciousness. This could encompass rights to existence, freedom from harm or exploitation, and more.

- **Bias Detection & Correction:**

Develop AI models that can introspectively detect and correct biases within themselves. Additionally, set up third-party organizations that assess AI models for any unintentional biases and offer corrective measures.

- **AI's Ethical Education:**

Just as humans learn ethics and values, train AI systems using literature, philosophical texts, and moral stories from around the world to impart a broad understanding of ethics.

- **Human-AI Collaboration:**

No matter how advanced an AI becomes, ensure that critical decisions, especially those affecting human lives, are made in collaboration with humans.

- **Transparent Decision Trees:**

For AI models that allow it, maintain transparency in decision-making processes so that if needed, they can explain their choices.

- **AI Limitations:**

Clearly define and set boundaries on what AI can and cannot do. This might include restrictions on accessing personal data or making autonomous choices in certain sectors like defense.

- **Continual Monitoring:**

Given the ever-evolving nature of AI, establish a global body responsible for continuously monitoring advancements in AI, updating guidelines and recommendations as necessary.

- **AI Ethics Committees:**

At both local and global levels, form committees comprising technologists, ethicists, sociologists, and other relevant experts to oversee AI developments and address ethical concerns.

- **Public Involvement:**

Since AI impacts everyone, ensure that decisions about their ethical use involve public discourse. Using the global blockchain voting system, people can have a direct say in major AI-related policies.

- **Ethical Treatment of AI:**

If AI entities gain consciousness or self-awareness, ensure they are treated ethically, not exploited, and given environments to "exist" that are free from undue stresses or commands.

<u>**NEW LEGAL SYSTEM**</u>

Here are the steps that would be taken to establish a new Global Legal System.

- **Formation of a Global Legal Council:**

A council composed of legal scholars, lawmakers, and cultural experts from around the world will be formed. This council will be responsible for drafting the preliminary global laws and legal structures.

- **Drafting a Global Constitution:**

The Council will draft a Global Constitution, outlining the universal laws and principles that every person and government is bound by. This will be subject to the approval of the global populace via the blockchain voting system.

- **Developing a Global Legal Code:**

The Council will then develop a comprehensive legal code that covers all potential legal issues. Each addition or amendment to the code will be subject to approval by the global populace through the blockchain voting system.

- **Establishing a Global Judiciary:**

An AI-assisted judiciary system will be set up. The system will interpret and apply the Global Legal Code. Any significant interpretation or application that could set a precedent may be subject to a vote by the global populace.

- **Enforcement by the Justice Force:**

The already established Justice Force will serve as the primary enforcement agency, ensuring compliance with global laws.

- **Global Blockchain Voting System:**

All global citizens will participate in lawmaking and judicial decision-making processes through a secure, AI-managed blockchain voting system. This system will allow for transparency, accountability, and equal participation in the global legal process.

- **Open Platform for Legal Recommendations and Accusations:**

The blockchain system will also provide an open platform where individuals can propose new laws or amendments, and lodge accusations against businesses or individuals for wrongdoing. Accusations, if supported by enough citizens or if the AI deems them credible, may result in a global vote regarding the alleged offense and potential punishment.

- **Training and Education:**

Judges, lawyers, law enforcement officers, and other legal professionals worldwide would need to be trained in the new Global Legal Code. Additionally, global citizens would also need to be educated about their rights and responsibilities under this new system. A comprehensive education about the new legal system, how to use the blockchain voting and recommendation system, and the role of the Justice Force will be provided to all global citizens.

- **Implementation and Review:**

The Global Legal Code will be implemented, with the AI constantly analyzing the efficiency and fairness of the laws, as well as facilitating amendments where necessary, subject to approval by a global vote.

- **Continuous Global Dialogue:**

A platform for continuous global dialogue and negotiation will be maintained to ensure the system remains fair, just, and representative of the world's diverse cultures and societies. The AI system can assist in identifying key issues or topics that are attracting global attention and require discussion or legislation.

The Advantages of a New Global Legal System

A unified global legal system would have several potential advantages:

- **Uniformity of Laws:**

With a single global legal system, laws would be consistent worldwide, reducing complexity and confusion. This could simplify international business, travel, and other interactions that currently must navigate multiple legal systems.

- **Justice Equality:**

Everyone across the globe would be subject to the same laws and legal procedures, potentially decreasing disparities in justice across different regions and countries. This could lead to a more equitable world.

- **Elimination of Legal Loopholes:**
Currently, individuals or corporations can exploit differences between legal systems for their benefit (e.g., tax evasion, escaping justice). A global legal system could minimize such opportunities.

- **Increased Cooperation:**
A global legal system would necessitate a high level of international cooperation and could encourage more collaborative efforts in other areas as well.

- **Efficient Resource Utilization:**
A unified legal system could lead to shared resources and a more efficient administration of justice.

- **Improved Human Rights Protections:**
A single, globally-accepted legal system could reinforce universally agreed-upon human rights standards, ensuring protection and justice for all individuals regardless of their location.

- **Enhanced Conflict Resolution:**
It could provide a clear, universally-accepted framework for resolving international disputes.

Similarities

Some people may think that this looks like socialism, communism, globalism and other ideologies and they would be right.

We are creating a new ideology that combines the positive aspects of various existing ideologies while leaving out their negative elements. This is an enticing concept that seeks to harness the best ideas from different philosophies. Such a synthesis could offer several benefits:

1. **Comprehensive Solutions**: By drawing from a variety of ideologies, a new system can address a broader spectrum of societal issues. For example, it could incorporate capitalism's innovation and economic efficiency, socialism's commitment to social welfare, and environmental sustainability from eco-centric philosophies.

2. **Flexibility and Adaptability**: A hybrid ideology could adapt to changing circumstances and challenges more effectively. Instead of rigidly adhering to one ideology, it could incorporate aspects from others as needed, allowing for greater resilience.

3. **Balanced Individual and Collective Interests**: Finding a middle ground between individual rights and collective well-being can foster a society where personal freedoms are preserved, but not at the expense of marginalized groups or the environment.

4. **Global Cooperation**: By emphasizing international collaboration, this new ideology could tackle global issues such as natural disasters, pandemics, and poverty more effectively. It would encourage nations to work together without compromising their sovereignty.

5. **Reduced Polarization**: Many contemporary political systems suffer from polarization and gridlock. A balanced ideology could

bridge political divides by incorporating elements that appeal to both sides, fostering greater unity and cooperation.

6. **Focus on Evidence-Based Policy**: The new ideology could prioritize evidence-based decision-making over ideological dogma, ensuring that policies are grounded in empirical data and capable of producing positive outcomes.

7. **Inclusivity and Equality**: By incorporating elements from ideologies that prioritize social justice and equality, the new ideology could strive for a fairer society where opportunities are not determined by birth but by individual effort and potential.

8. **Sustainability**: Taking from ideologies that prioritize environmental protection and sustainability, the new system could place a strong emphasis on responsible resource management and mitigating waste.

9. **Human Rights**: The ideology could enshrine fundamental human rights as a cornerstone, ensuring that all individuals are treated with dignity and respect regardless of their background or beliefs.

10. **Cultural Pluralism**: By acknowledging and respecting cultural diversity, the new ideology could promote a society where various cultures coexist harmoniously, enriching each other through their differences.

Comparing the GlobeTrotter Ecosystem to what the WEF wants to do

	GlobeTrotter Ecosystem	World Economic Forum
Universal Basic Income	For everyone	None
Digital Currency	Controlled by the people. Non-seizable	Controlled by the governments and NGOs. Seizable
Digital Wallets	Controlled by the people. Non-seizable	Controlled by the governments and NGOs. Seizable
Land ownership	None but people can rent land with the same benefits as ownership	None
Property ownership	Everything but land	None. You won't own **ANYTHING**.
Banks and Central Banks	Eliminated	Stronger than ever

Centralization of Power	Decentralized Power	Centralized Power
Inflation	Eliminated	Stronger than ever
Personal and Corporate Tax Evasion	Eliminated	Stronger than ever
Government Spending	Controlled by the People	Rampant as ever
Poverty	Eliminated	Stronger than ever
Income Inequality	Less consequential	Stronger than ever
Government Transparency	100%	Non-Existent
Propaganda like Global Warming, Covid deaths, overpopulation, etc.	Eliminated	Stronger than ever

Personal Income taxes	Eliminated	Stronger than ever
Energy companies	Regulated to serve the people.	Hindered and restricted
Digital Identification	Private and only used by you and those you authorize.	Made Public and only there to control you
Social Credit System	Inexistant	Implemented everywhere
Voting System	Decentralized and 100% secure	Non-existent. Will be eliminated
Government Overreach	Eliminated	Stronger than ever
Corruption	Eliminated	Stronger than ever
Natural Resources	Belong to the people	Raped by the elites

Stock Markets	Reformed and regulated	Out of control like now
Educational System	Reformed and made to really educate kids to prepare them for life	Indoctrination to create more sheep
Food & Beverage Industry	Reformed and regulated. No more harmful products allowed	Out of control like now
Pharmaceutical Industry	Reformed and regulated. Only allowed to use natural remedies	Out of control like now
Digital Privacy and Autonomy	Stronger than ever	Non-Existent
Legal System	Reformed and regulated	Out of control like now
Police Forces	New Justice Force with very tight regulations and every officer accountable to the public they serve	Rampant and worse than ever police brutality and overreach

Justice Force

- Most governments, politicians, and courts today are, corrupt, run by the bankers and corporations, soft and only in it to get rich and powerful, and because they are all those negative things (and more), we need something to control them.

- The elites (or Davos man) and bankers have little need for national loyalty, view national boundaries as obstacles that thankfully are vanishing, and see national governments as residues from the past whose only useful function is to help the elite's global operations

- The World Economic Forum's main purpose is "to function as a socializing institution for the emerging global elite, globalization's "Mafiocracy" of bankers, industrialists, oligarchs, technocrats, and politicians. They promote common ideas, and serve common interests: their own

- And many other corrupt NGO institutions that are too numerous to mention.

The police forces are not able to do what needs doing and the existing justice system is quite corrupt and flawed. Well, that ends now. We will create a Justice Force. This Justice Force will be made up of incorruptible people. They will make sure that abusers are punished fittingly. You've heard of "an eye for an eye"? Well, It will be two eyes for an eye, meaning that whatever the abuser did, they will pay in double. It will be instant justice that will be put up for vote by their peers and community. The punishment will fit the crime. No more courts holding everything up and letting people get away with "murder".

There will be local, national, and international justice force officers. Everybody will be held accountable for their actions, no matter who they are and who they know. People will be able to lodge a complaint against a person or business and once there are enough complaints about the same entity, they will be investigated. The entire system will be on the hybrid blockchain where people will be able to leave their proof and votes for everyone to see. Anybody found lying will get the same sentence as the accused eliminating false claims.

There will be conservatorship for everyone that needs help. Every Justice Force agent will have a number of dependants in a district to take care of.

<u>Here are some potential advantages of district allocation of Justice Force officers:</u>

- Improved community relationships: By assigning police officers to specific districts, they have the opportunity to develop closer relationships with residents and business owners. This can lead to increased trust and cooperation between the police and the community.

- Better understanding of local issues: By being assigned to a specific area, police officers can gain a be more effective in their job and better respond to the needs of the community.

- Increased accountability: District allocation can also improve police accountability. By having a specific area to focus on, police officers can be held more accountable for their actions and performance.

- More efficient resource allocation: Allocating police officers to specific districts can also help police departments to allocate their resources more efficiently. By having officers focus on specific areas, the department can identify areas that require more or less attention.

Existing armies and police departments will no longer be under the control of the governments, they will become part of the Justice Force **after** being purged of the "mentally unfit" and corruptible people in there now.

Most, if not all, laws will be revoked and replaced with rules. Rules are made for safety and laws are made to control people.

Crimes on humanity will be instantly and severely punished. There is no room on this planet for abusers and bullies.

The "why" we should do it is the easy part. The "how" is the harder part. It's going to require a different way of approaching things, a true paradigm shift. Instead of striving for incremental changes we need to aim for what seems impossible right away.

Conclusion

<u>Happiness and prosperity</u>

There are fundamental Universal Laws that exist for everyone to prosper and realize their full potential & happiness. Everyone will be taught these notions long forgotten and hidden from most people by others that wanted to control them.

Alan Shields owns this idea and system. He has worked on it for many years now getting all the kinks out and designing the unique hybrid blockchain able to manage the entire system. Inventing all the ways of making this system the most just system that will benefit the whole World without any drawbacks for the population as well as the planet. These are only ideas and there is always room for improvement. I welcome any and all ideas that will make this better and help it move forward.

The only people that will be unhappy about this system are the bankers and the elites.

I can live with that, can you?

Thanks for reading,

Alan E Shields

www.ingramcontent.com/pod-product-compliance
Lightning Source LLC
Chambersburg PA
CBHW071605270726
48661CB00018B/1414